TOUGHLOVE
FAMILIES TALK ABOUT
TOUGHLOVE

BROOKLYN, NY

"TOUGHLOVE saved my life, and that's the truth. What happened when we went there is that we found out that we weren't alone—and we got support."

LONG ISLAND, NY

"The main thing TOUGHLOVE does is give parents back some of their self-esteem. It gives us the courage to continue to take a stand and stick to it."

TEENAGER, DOYLESTOWN, PA

"TOUGHLOVE helped my parents understand what I was going through, and I could understand what they were going through. We can talk now, and we really get along."

TRUANT OFFICER, KANE COUNTY, IL

"It's such a help for these parents. Parents go from feeling utterly hopeless to ten feet tall."

CHICAGO, IL

"It has really helped a great deal to bring peace and harmony to the family. It makes kids responsible for their actions."

TOUGHLOVE®

Phyllis and David York and Ted Wachtel

BANTAM BOOKS
NEW YORK · TORONTO · LONDON · SYDNEY · AUCKLAND

*This edition contains the complete text
of the original hardcover edition.*
NOT ONE WORD HAS BEEN OMITTED.

TOUGHLOVE®

*A Bantam Book / published by arrangement with
Doubleday*

PRINTING HISTORY

*Doubleday edition published October 1982
A Selection of Literary Guild
Serialized in Doubleday Syndicate
Bantam edition / October 1983
10 printings through February 1990*

ISBN 0-553-23695-4

Published simultaneously in the United States and Canada

Bantam Books are published by Bantam Books, a division of Bantam
Doubleday Dell Publishing Group, Inc. Its trademark, consisting of the
words "Bantam Books" and the portrayal of a rooster, is Registered in U.S.
Patent and Trademark Office and in other countries. Marca Registrada.
Bantam Books, 666 Fifth Avenue, New York, New York 10103.

PRINTED IN THE UNITED STATES OF AMERICA

H   16   15   14   13   12   11   10

CONTENTS

TOUGHLOVE

Part I

THE TOUGHLOVE PROBLEM

Chapter 1

The Problem

The gray marble waiting room of the Los Angeles Juvenile Court is filled with parents and their children. Inside the courtroom, lanky fifteen-year-old Robert and his parents stand before the judge. Robert is surly and inattentive while his parents seem angry and embarrassed. He hangs his head and appears to listen to the magistrate's lecture and the setting of the fine. His parents, who have already paid truancy and disorderly conduct fines, helplessly pay his underage drinking fine. As they leave the courtroom the next family enters for a repeat performance.

On Friday morning Barbara's mom is aware of her daughter's evasive behavior and that familiar blank look on her face. Barbara received two telephone calls late last night and refuses to talk about them or anything else this morning. Barbara rushes to leave their comfortable Mobile, Alabama, home in order to catch her ride to school. Barbara's mom senses what is coming. Sixteen-year-old Barbara is about to take off again. She will be gone anywhere from two days to three weeks, perhaps more. Helplessly Mom starts to cry.

3

In Queens, New York, Tom, age sixty-two, is waking up his twenty-seven-year-old son, Frank. Tom shakes Frank by the arm and says, "Frank, Frank, come on, get up. You'll be late for that job interview I arranged." Frank angrily jerks his arm away, gets out of bed in a rage, and puts his fist through the wallboard that Tom recently replaced.

Frank starts screaming, "Leave me the fuck alone. I don't want no charity job. You know I'm sick. I see a damn shrink because of all the problems I had as a kid." Tom leaves the room dismayed and frightened by the violent outburst.

Tom goes to the kitchen to tell his wife, Helen, what happened and warn her that Frank is in one of his violent moods again. On the way he checks the medicine chest and notes that all of Frank's pills are gone and it is three days until his next psychiatrist's appointment. Tom knows that without the medication Frank is going to be very difficult to live with.

Tom tells Helen and comments about how he wishes the two of them could run away and hide. Helen tearfully replies, "Yes, but he is our son and he really needs us. He always had trouble, even as a little boy. He really needs us to stand by him now. We're all he's got. Even his brothers and sisters won't have him around anymore."

Frank, fully dressed, enters the kitchen and asks his dad for ten dollars so he can try and make the job interview anyway. Tom contritely gives his son twenty dollars and tells him to get something to eat later. As Frank leaves, Tom and Helen wearily sit in the kitchen feeling defeated, depressed, and angry. They both hope he will get a job this time that will put him on the right track.

Margo stops at the mailbox at the end of the driveway of her Duluth home. She is surprised by a letter that informs her that her eleven-year-old, Jason, has only been in school two days out of the last two weeks. Margo is sure there is some mistake because she drove Jason to school every day and watched him enter. But a nagging doubt takes hold of her. If what this letter says is true, then what is her son doing all day? Where does he go? Margo begins to get frightened. Her husband left two years ago and she feels trapped and alone as a single parent and sole provider for the family. Margo nervously enters her apartment.

Ronnie, a pretty woman of thirty, works full-time in a local department store and lives at home. Her parents are uncomfortable about their relationship with Ronnie, although their reasons are somewhat vague. Ronnie is not on drugs, stealing, or getting into any trouble, but she is rarely at home and does not pay the agreed upon rent or upkeep on the family car she uses. A few weeks ago the bank called about overdue payments on Ronnie's loan, for which they cosigned. Ronnie insisted that it was a mistake and that she would straighten out the matter. But today a letter comes from the bank threatening collection proceedings unless payments are made immediately. Reluctantly they make out a check and mail it to the bank.

In a Toronto hospital emergency room, twenty-two-year-old Marvin lies unconscious from a drug overdose. A nurse attempts to question the sleazy-looking group that brought Marvin to the hospital about the drugs that he had ingested, but they refuse to answer any questions and leave the hospital. The emergency room staff frantically looks for clues, hoping they will get lucky again, for this is not the first time that they have struggled to bring Marvin back from the brink of death.

Dennis and Roland's parents are watching television in the family room of their Brockton, Massachusetts, split-level home. As usual, Roland's stereo is blasting through the house. Dad can no longer stand the noise so he marches upstairs and yells, "Turn that damn thing down." Eighteen-year-old Roland responds immediately by screaming, "Fuck you," and he begins smashing in the walls of his room with a baseball bat. Sixteen-year-old Dennis charges into the hallway hollering at his father, "What the hell are you doing to my brother? Why don't you leave him alone?"

A widowed mother is talking to her Evanston, Illinois, parish priest about her nineteen-year-old adopted son. "Father, I don't know what to do about Richard. He's stolen me blind. I don't have a TV anymore and he even took a small brooch that was all I had left of my mother's things. I have a padlock on my bedroom door and I don't dare leave my purse around. I've called the police but they tell me it's a family problem. I don't know where to turn. It's like living in hell." The priest has heard many such stories. He reaches over and pats her hand.

Near Burlington, Vermont, twenty-one-year-old Lynne is comforting her seventeen-year-old sister, Terri. Terri is crying hysterically about an argument she just had with her boyfriend. Terri gets up and goes to the bathroom. When she does not return, Lynne goes to find her.

Staring in horror, she is stunned by the blood running from Terri's wrists.

Jennifer, age fourteen, has been in therapy for the past eight months. Jennifer was referred to the psychiatrist by the school because she was found with marijuana in her purse and had been repeatedly truant. The psychiatrist feels she has been making progress because Jennifer has been talking to her openly about her drug use and the problems she is having at home. But now the psychiatrist is surprised when Jennifer's parents call to report that Jennifer did not come home last night and when they called the school they were told that she had not been in school all week. They ask the psychiatrist what they should do.

And so the stories go, from Youngstown to the Yukon, New York to New Orleans. Outrageous and destructive behavior in our young people whose ages range from teens to thirties. In our cities and suburbs and small rural towns.

Despite the wide geographical dispersion, the behaviors our children exhibit are amazingly similar. And so are the excuses they offer to justify the turmoil and frustration that they cause all around themselves.

In their homes they are:

Living in filthy bedrooms and saying that it is their room and they can do what they want.

Leaving dirty dishes around and claiming that they did not do it.

Fighting with their siblings and saying that their brothers and sisters started it.

Fighting with their parents and saying that Mom or Dad was nagging them.

Consistently coming home late and saying they forgot the time, ran out of gas, their watch was slow.

Stealing objects from their homes and denying it.

Stealing money from parents, grandparents, brothers, and sisters and denying it.

Bringing home rude, unkempt people and blaming the family for making their friends feel uncomfortable.

Playing their stereos at all hours and at ear-shattering levels and claiming they were only listening to music.

Coming home drunk or stoned frequently and saying they were just partying.

Breaking doors, walls, and furniture and claiming that they just got angry and could not control themselves.

Avoiding other family members and claiming that their family does not understand them.

Lying around the house all day and staying out all night and saying that they cannot find a job.

Concerning school issues they are:

Getting suspended because teachers are hassling them.

Playing hooky because school is boring and they want to get a job.

Fighting with teachers because they accuse them falsely.

Failing because teachers have it in for them, school is boring, and they have a learning disability.

Not bringing home their report card because they forgot it, lost it, owe money to the library.

Concerning employment issues they are:

Getting fired because the boss was hassling them.

Quitting jobs because they are boring.

Not having money for bills because they did not get paid, lost the money, owed the money to others.

Not getting jobs or job interviews because they forgot, overslept, had the wrong time, could not find the place, did not have carfare.

Concerning legal issues they are:

Getting fined for disorderly conduct even though the other people started it.

Getting tickets for driving offenses because the policeman did not like them.

Having accidents which were caused by other drivers.

Being accused of robbery even though they were just standing there watching.

Being accused of dealing dope when they were just holding it for someone else.

Shoplifting because the stores charge too much.

Such shoddy behavior and still shoddier excuses are a growing reality for parents, schools, police, and courts throughout North America. Social service agencies and detention centers are overflowing with acting-out, destructive young people who seem to have no sense of limits or propriety.

Our schools have tried special classes, stiffer punishments, or intensive counseling, but to no avail. Drug abuse on school premises has become commonplace, as have assaults on teachers. Many schools have given up on these young people as students and simply expel them when they can.

Our police, probation officers, and judges are overwhelmed by the number of juvenile offenders. Costly rehabilitation or counseling programs do not seem to yield many positive results, nor does costly incarceration.

Nor have our social service agencies and professional counselors stemmed the tide. Many have taken to hiding behind intimidating technical jargon, naming the problem adolescent adjustment neurosis, sociopathic personality, early childhood trauma, and low self-esteem. But what that really means is they do not know what to do.

Most frustrated of all are parents. We feel responsible for our children's behavior. We search our own actions, conscious or unconscious, for the cause. Perhaps there was psychological trauma in important developmental stages, perhaps divorce, remarriage, the death of a loved one. Perhaps faulty genes, lack of vitamins, too much sugar. We try medical solutions, taking our son or daughter to various doctors to find a cure. Or we try counseling, spending hundreds, even thousands of dollars on one therapy after another.

Parents feel ashamed, guilty, and blamed. Family stress and anxiety increase with each escalating incident and failed solution. The other children avoid being home or stay in their rooms. The family is filled with anger, fear, frustration, hurt, and especially helplessness.

Helplessness that is mirrored by our society at large. Helplessness that has developed because the solutions of the past are not working and will not work on the problems young people are creating for themselves, their families, and their communities. The kind of helplessness that the people of Hamelin felt as the Pied Piper marched off with their children. We watch, immobilized, as our children and young adults willingly dance to the tune of their own self-destruction.

But their dance is not only self-destructive. A young person disrupting a class is interfering with the lives of all the other students, a drunk or drugged driver is dangerous to others on the road, and an unruly son or daughter creates turmoil for all the members of the family.

The effects on the family can be devastating. Marriages can be threatened as arguments and blame between parents increase with each new development. Otherwise healthy families can be torn asunder by the emotional upheaval and disruption.

The assumption made by many, that something must be wrong in the first place with the family of a young person who behaves like this, is erroneous. The notion that children must be neglected, deprived, and abused to become mean and nasty is fundamentally incorrect.

Our destructive young people come from all kinds of home environments. Their parents are white, black, yellow, or brown; rich, poor, or middle class; educated or uneducated; permissive or strict; deeply religious of every faith or uninvolved in any faith; divorced, remarried, or still in their first marriage. The young people themselves are first born, second born, eighth born, only child, or adopted. And rarely are all the children in one family acting out. Usually one or two are disrupting the lives of the others in the family.

The common denominator is rotten behavior. Despite a wide range of geographical, social, and economic backgrounds, our young people behave with stereotypical predictability. Like clones stamped out in some satanic laboratory, they share an underlying selfishness and similar ways of demonstrating it.

If this youthful destructive behavior were a manifestation of individual family problems or pathology, then the dilemma would be manageable. We could simply muster enough resources, family therapists, drug rehabilitation centers, and counseling programs, and the numbers of acting-out youth would be reduced. But exactly the opposite is true. Looking for family problems and pathology which "cause" this behavior distracts from the real issue: the responsibility of each young person for his or her own actions.

The pursuit of "causes" outside the individual person is our current cultural preoccupation. Fostered by the popularization of psychological notions, we are mired in finding reasons for unacceptable behavior instead of setting limits on what is acceptable and demanding that unacceptable behavior stop.

That is not to say that therapists, rehabilitation centers, and counseling programs are useless. But without a clear focus on the real responsibility for problem behavior, by getting distracted in blaming parents or other "causes," we are largely wasting our resources.

Our cultural dilemma needs a cultural solution. We need to shed our misconceptions and redefine our strategies. Without blame. Without malice. Cooperatively. Moving in a new direction to insist that our young people accept the consequences for their negative actions. Parents, teachers, police, probation officers, caseworkers, therapists, judges, citizens in general. Together. Providing a tough but loving solution for our tragic contemporary problem. That is what TOUGHLOVE is all about.

Chapter 2

The Solution

TOUGHLOVE is a program for parents troubled by unaccetable "teenage" behavior. That does not limit the program to parents of teenagers, for many young people in their twenties and thirties have failed to make the transition to adulthood and have much the same dependency on their parents as teenagers do.

Fundamental to TOUGHLOVE is the parent/community support group. The parent/community support group brings together the parents of these young people to help each other learn to look at their problem differently and gradually change their responses to their children's behavior. The group also reaches out to the schools, the legal system, and to human service agencies and professionals to develop a common understanding of TOUGHLOVE's purposes and strategies and to achieve a cooperative approach to this pressing social dilemma.

The TOUGHLOVE process enables parents, with support, to begin to confront their son's or daughter's behavior. This means putting aside their guesses about hidden motivation and psychological reasons and taking a clear look at their intolerable child. The difficulty with this seemingly simple first step is that by the time most

15

parents have come to TOUGHLOVE they have tried many different solutions without much success and need help in determining what is the real behavior they need to confront and what are some small steps they can manage in the beginning.

People, it may seem, should be able to do this by themselves. But experience has demonstrated that they cannot, and one of the most powerful and helpful elements of TOUGHLOVE is support. Support from people who understand and empathize. Support from people who do not come on as superior authorities with magical solutions. So many parents have been pushed into deeper states of guilt and helplessness by, at best, ineffectual, well-meaning experts or, at worst, by experts who perceive the parents of acting-out youth as hurtful and uncaring and in turn treat parents in hurtful and uncaring ways. People who have not experienced the problem have difficulty understanding the trauma and confusion.

In the beginning of the process most TOUGHLOVE parents feel the same way about support. They are embarrassed to take the help of others. After some experience with getting and giving support, it feels so good that parents wonder how they ever got along without it.

Most of the support is quite simple, like making a telephone call or inviting someone to have a cup of coffee and chat for a few minutes. Other ways TOUGH-LOVE group members are supportive is in helping parents deal with community resources effectively, for example, by going with another parent to schools, police departments, courts, or social service agencies.

Most parents, when they deal with these community agencies, are so upset that they do not hear, understand, do not ask good questions, get defensive, angry, or frightened, and generally fail to achieve a cooperative atmosphere. At these times many parents are so embarrassed and guilt-ridden that they just want to escape from the situation. But with the support of others the experience can be productive. The support parent can get the information necessary to start the proper action. Parents, working together, can get help and develop cooperative plans that will move the problem toward some resolution instead of falling into destructive patterns.

The TOUGHLOVE group members can also help parents enlist their own families in the effort, instead of hiding the problem from the rest of their family or feeling blamed by them. Grandparents, aunts, uncles, brothers, and sisters can all help when they become attuned to the TOUGHLOVE strategies.

Two real-life examples help illustrate support and how it works when families and communities cooperate effectively to help young people experience consequences for negative behavior:

Jenny's mom and dad were very concerned that she was smoking dope and taking other drugs. A pleasant girl and good student, she had changed lately, becoming moody and doing poorly in school. They joined a TOUGHLOVE group and began to challenge their daughter's behavior.

First they talked to Jenny about her behavior and suggested getting help but she ignored their suggestions. Then they asked members of the TOUGHLOVE group to sit in with them when they talked to her. Finally they decided to take more drastic action.

Supported by members of their group, they decided to share their problem with other people in their very large family, inviting them to help. Jenny awoke one morning to shocked grandparents and angry aunts and uncles, all gathered in her bedroom, holding the marijuana and smoking paraphernalia they had just found. One can only imagine her reaction to the bizarre scene.

This confrontation was repeated on an irregular basis for three weeks. Although Jenny's irate anger was intense, her family persisted. The behavior that concerned her parents stopped and her school work improved. Her anger subsided and there have been no further problems. Jenny said, "How the hell could I keep doing it if they were going to tell my grandmother every time?"

Although behavioral changes are not usually accomplished so quickly, this situation demonstrates the result of a little creativity and a sense of humor. The fringe benefit for the parents was the wonderful close and caring feeling which developed between their TOUGHLOVE group friends and themselves, people they had not known before. The second fringe benefit was the sense of support they felt from their own relatives.

It seems like such a simple thing to invite family members in to help with a problem, but it goes against much of our parental pride and false independence. Grandparents and other relatives who have become involved with parents in our TOUGHLOVE groups are deeply concerned and very much value being offered the opportunity to help their loved ones, but it often takes the support and encouragement of group members for parents to take that leap of faith needed to involve their own family.

The second anecdote is a perfect example of the power of community cooperation:

Pamela, a fourteen-year-old who was on court probation for numerous shoplifting offenses, left for school and did not return. This was a familiar pattern since she had run away several times, once staying away for a month. As usual her parents were distraught with fear and her brother and sister were resentful and told them to forget about her. "Pam's just no good and we're all better off without her."

The parents had recently joined a local TOUGHLOVE parent/community support group so they brought the problem up at their weekly meeting, with Pam now missing for the second day. This particular group had been in existence for many months and had developed an effective working relationship with the local schools, police, children and youth agency, and juvenile court. Group members proposed the following strategy and the parents willingly agreed.

The next morning two group members went to the local police station with the runaway daughter's address book. They asked the police to check at the homes of Pam's friends and if they found her to bring her to juvenile court. Meanwhile Pam's father called his daughter's probation officer and requested her assistance in setting up a hearing at juvenile court if Pam was located. Pam's caseworker at the children and youth agency was also contacted about the hearing and invited to attend when Pam was found. The TOUGH-LOVE group had done its work in previous months and achieved an understanding with juvenile court that informal hearings could be scheduled whenever needed, so all the community resources were mobilized to deal with Pam.

The police began to make their inquiries and within an hour Pam called her parents saying that she wanted to come home. Pam, of course, heard about the police involvement from one of her friends whose home had been called and became frightened. Her mother told Pam that two parents from the TOUGHLOVE group would pick her up in a half hour. She then called the probation officer at juvenile court and the children and youth caseworker. The scene was now set.

Pam was taken to juvenile court where the entire entourage, including a family worker for the court, met with her. She was informed that she was to begin attending school regularly, a condition that would be checked by one of the TOUGHLOVE parents daily, that she was to return home promptly after school each day, a condition that would be checked by her probation officer, and that she was to meet weekly with her caseworker from the children and youth agency. Pam was informed that if this was not agreeable to her or if she violated the requirements, she would be sent to a foster home in a distant part of the state. Reluctantly Pam signed the contract and the family worker took the document into the office of a judge who signed it.

Although the hearing was unofficial and the judge's signature was only symbolic, Pam was impressed. Never had she been faced with such consequences for her behavior. Never had her parents seemed so determined and well-supported. Never had so many official people faced her so forcefully.

That event occurred six months ago as of this writing and Pam has not run away or shoplifted since. She has actually become friendly with one of the families in her parents' TOUGHLOVE group and spends time at the family's home. Her own family is still fearful but everyone has been attending counseling sessions and the parents report that they have a much nicer family situation now.

What makes this such a perfect example of TOUGH-LOVE's potential is the way in which the community pitched in to help Pam and her family. It took a cooperative group of people focusing a lot of energy and trust on this one occasion, rather than many separate agencies working for years in the usual fashion. The TOUGHLOVE group had worked long and hard to make this cooperative community possible and as a result it is a better place for everyone.

The Community Service Foundation of Sellersville, Pennsylvania, TOUGHLOVE's sponsoring agency, is fostering the development of parent/community support groups and there are now hundreds of such groups in the United States and Canada. Given the rapid growth of TOUGHLOVE and the widespread attention it has received in print and on broadcast media, many people have heard about TOUGHLOVE but their understanding is largely superficial. Therefore it is important to dispel some of the popular misconceptions about TOUGHLOVE. Indeed, one way of knowing what something is, is to know what it is *not*.

TOUGHLOVE is *not* a child-rearing program. Although TOUGHLOVE concepts may have some implications for child rearing, TOUGHLOVE is directed toward young people whose outrageous behavior requires unorthodox responses.

TOUGHLOVE is *not* a quickie solution but a gradual process that helps parents move out of the helpless position and feelings that have overtaken them. Through a sequence of small action steps parents make their acting-out young person responsible for the consequences of his or her unacceptable behavior.

TOUGHLOVE does *not* encourage parents to "throw their kid out of the house." Only after other alternatives are attempted is an acting-out youth faced with a *structured choice* to change his or her behavior or leave. In such situations other parents in the group offer temporary housing or arrangements are made with the appropriate social service agencies. Often the youth will "take to the streets" for a while but he or she is provided with telephone numbers of group members so that an orderly return can be arranged.

TOUGHLOVE is *not* a way for parents to give up responsibility for their children forever, either economically or emotionally. TOUGHLOVE strategies are directed toward achieving reconciliation of the child with his or her family, even if it takes a very long time.

TOUGHLOVE is *not* a way to get a young person to be loving toward his or her parents. For a family in crisis the goal is cooperation first, and perhaps togetherness will come later.

TOUGHLOVE is *not* a return to the dictum "spare the rod and spoil the child." TOUGHLOVE groups help parents brainstorm creative alternatives to the use of force and encourage the involvement of the police whenever parents or other family members are threatened by violence.

Most significantly, TOUGHLOVE is *not* a method for a single set of parents, all by themselves, to solve their own problem. The support and involvement of others, family, friends, and TOUGHLOVE group members, are critical. Without active support from others, troubled parents are almost surely doomed to failure in their efforts.

We (the Yorks) know because we developed TOUGH-LOVE from personal experience, from the trauma of dealing with our own teenage daughters' unacceptable behavior. Our family's dilemma fell upon us like a dead weight and crushed our old perceptions of parental roles, forcing us to reevaluate who we thought we were, how we were raising our kids, where our ideas came from, and where they led us. At the end of a long, hard journey of self-confrontation we found new ideas which became the basis for TOUGHLOVE.

Not until we looked at many other families in our own private practice, at the drug rehabilitation program where we worked part-time, and in some of the early TOUGHLOVE groups were we able to formulate a clear philosophy for TOUGHLOVE. We have summarized our philosophy in what we call the Ten Beliefs. Although we didn't find them on the mountain and they aren't chiseled in stone, they can serve as a kind of Ten Commandments for troubled parents. The Ten Beliefs are as follows:

1. Family problems have roots and supports in the culture.
2. Parents are people too.
3. Parents' material and emotional resources are limited.
4. Parents and kids are not equal.
5. Blaming keeps people helpless.
6. Kids' behavior affects parents. Parents' behavior affects kids.
7. Taking a stand precipitates a crisis.
8. From controlled crisis comes positive change.
9. Families need to give and get support in their own community in order to change.
10. The essence of family life is cooperation, not togetherness.

We use terms like "kids" which we find intimate and friendly in the Ten Beliefs, in our work as trainers, and in this book to relax people who are often intimidated by the formal jargon of many professionals. TOUGHLOVE is a cultural solution that depends on parents, professionals, and other community members cooperatively rejecting destructive behavior and supporting new patterns of behavior. There is no secret knowledge involved. Both lay people and professionals can attack the current dilemma when armed with new ways of looking at it and when equipped with the appropriate skills.

Part II

THE TEN BELIEFS

Chapter 3

Roots in the Culture

We learned the traditional psychological theories in our training as drug and alcohol abuse counselors and family therapists, but we came to question many of those ideas and how they are applied when we found ourselves on the other side of the counseling session in the role of troubled parents. Ross Fishman, for instance, Director of Education and Training for the New York affiliate of the National Council on Alcoholism, has suggested "that an adolescent's alcohol abuse is frequently a reaction to and a reflection of existing family dysfunction and that abusive drinking for the adolescent may serve as a means of calling attention to a family situation or crisis so as to provoke the family to recognize and to resolve it." (National Institute of Alcohol and Alcohol Abuse Information Feature Service, July 30, 1981.)

Being counselors ourselves, we subscribed to that kind of reasoning, so when we had problems with our daughters we went to family therapists to find our dysfunction. Instead we found that we only prolonged the problems by looking for the causes in our family's behavior, but made progress when we confronted their behavior. Some might suggest that we are simply rationalizing to avoid responsibility, but the positive results that we have achieved in our own family and with others belie that sort of explanation.

The theories of family dynamics that have been popularized in our culture have their origins in work with so-called schizophrenics and their families. It's our contention that the techniques and ideas are being applied inappropriately to families that are currently experiencing difficulty with their teenagers and young adults. And applied with little success. Most of the young people who are manifesting outrageous behavior today are not "crazy," they are "stoned." Searching for the roots of the problem in family history and dynamics is largely unproductive.

The theories simply do not reflect the changes that have swept through our way of life in recent decades. As the first of the Ten Beliefs states, "Family problems have roots and supports in the culture." And our culture is changing at a staggering pace. Looking back to the sixties and seventies brings a blur of images to mind. Lost or fallen heroes. Challenges to traditional ideals, values, and authority. New technology and new lifestyles.

Even the word "lifestyle" is new. When David was growing up, earning a living and fighting World War II were the most pressing issues. People didn't have the luxury of deciding which lifestyle to pursue, or at least they didn't perceive a choice. But the culture is different now.

Born in 1929, David was as much influenced by the Great Depression as by his family. In fact it literally brought about the disintegration of his family. David's father was in real estate and the crashing economy quickly destroyed his livelihood and his morale. David found himself in a foster care facility, an awesome life change for a small boy.

By today's standards David would have been "justified" in expressing his emotional frustrations through destructive behavior. He could have abused drugs, skipped school, and raised all kinds of hell, but there were no supports in the culture for acting out. Instead, like many others at this time, David denied and repressed his feelings. The era in which a person lives defines the kinds of problems he experiences and the solutions that are available.

David remembers that he was impressed by things like the cartoons of the time which showed the homeless men or hoboes who were always stealing pies left by housewives to cool on windowsills. The important people were policemen and school teachers because they had good jobs. "Making it" by going to college so dominated his thoughts that overt rebellion and destruction were out of the question.

Phyllis is eight years younger than David and the events of World War II predominate in her early childhood recollections. Being Jewish, she was horrified by the newsreels of the Nazi concentration camps and especially her European cousins' own agonizing stories of torture, starvation, and the death of loved ones.

She remembers making friends with a Jewish girl, newly arrived from Holland, and learning how the girl's father had died before the war and her mother had remarried a non-Jewish man. She told Phyllis that her stepfather's non-Jewish status had enabled them to escape. In Phyllis's teens when she dated non-Jewish boys and ultimately married David, her parents agonized about what they had done wrong. As she later realized, it had absolutely nothing to do with her parents or what they had done. She simply felt a need to be safe from the threatening world of her past and that need outweighed the influence of her family.

As a teenager in the early fifties, Phyllis also felt the influence of the growing youth subculture. But drag racing, drinking, and balling in the backseat were considered the limits of outrageous teen behavior in that decade. On the pop level obscenity was Elvis Presley shaking his hips while promiscuity and pregnancy were unspoken evils. For a few musicians, artists, poor people, and beatniks, marijuana and heroin were available, a mere hint of the current glut. James Dean, the "rebel without a cause," was the forerunner of today's adolescent antihero, victimized and misunderstood by idiotic parents.

Since James Dean's time we have increasingly focused on teenagers' feelings, especially their "sad" and "bad" feelings, which has led us to one of psychiatry's most pervasive contributions to modern culture, the victim. We have absorbed through our collective cultural skins psychological notions about the normality of oedipal conflict, that it is expected and acceptable for children to want to destroy at least one parent. Acceptance of a kid's aggression and rebellion against parents has expanded to include authority in general. We have been encouraged to "understand" these psychological developmental principles and been told that our understanding will solve everything. In fact, if we all take the latest "parenting" courses our understanding will *prevent* everything.

When a sensational case of rape, assassination, murder, or child abuse occurs the initial horror soon turns to asking, "What went wrong in this person's life to make

him or her commit that crime?" The defense's witness,
a certified psychiatrist, points out the shortcomings of
the poor wretch's upbringing and how he or she was
mistreated by parents. We feel sorry for the perpetrator,
angry with the parents, and we forget, at least for the
moment, the real victim.

As a high school student David once got in trouble
for passing a note containing "obscenities." After school
the understanding teacher told how he and his wife
liked to help "kids from broken homes." As soon as the
teacher said that David realized he could "get over" on
the guy. He made David a victim and handed him a
perfect excuse for inappropriate behavior: a broken
home.

Ironically our cultural perceptions have not caught
up with the realities of modern life and we are overrun
by victims. In the forties when psychological theories
began to influence people like David's teacher, so-called
broken homes were uncommon. In the seventies and
eighties half the marriages end in divorce. Do all the
children from these marriages get to be excused as
"kids from broken homes"? Or do we recognize the
new realities, that the majority of American families
experience divorce or include two working parents? We
can no longer afford to excuse so much of our children's
unacceptable behavior with psychological claptrap.

Working parents or divorced parents are not people
who "don't care about their kids." A great many social
and economic factors have brought us to the present
situation and whether we like it or not, most American
families are *not* comprised of a "breadwinner" dad and
a "housewife" mom who are married until "death do us
part." Single moms, single dads, moms living with a
man, dads living with a woman, or even gay parents are

all part of the current reality. In order to cope effectively with the dilemma of destructive young people, we must accept who we really are and not who we used to be or wish we could be. Then we can build societal structures which fit us.

Much of the unruly behavior experienced in today's families can be traced to the impact of the sixties and seventies. The antiwar movement of the Vietnam era, for instance, and the impeachment hearings of the Watergate era confirmed our already skeptical attitude toward authoritarian leaders. What was torn down has not been replaced and an air of cynicism and disrespect for authority persists. Police, teachers, and parents are no longer held in such high regard as they once were, for we have thrown out authority along with authoritarianism.

We remember the excitement of the sixties at Goddard, an experimental college in rural Vermont where Phyllis studied psychology and David taught biology. There was a parade of interesting people through our family's life including a mime troupe that stayed at our home and left a classic sixties message on our daughter's bedroom ceiling. It said, "Drop out before you're eight."

The popularity of dope also grew out of those decades and gained respectability as people challenged the "establishment" by blatantly smoking reefer on the White House lawn. The sincerity of conviction which accompanied those acts of defiance has since faded to self-serving hedonism. No longer a political act, the use of dope supports a multibillion-dollar business, one of the most lucrative industries in America.

Widespread drug use and abuse has fostered an atmosphere in our society much like that of Prohibition years. Besides putting huge fortunes into the hands of smugglers and distributors, the illegal status of the popular substances has made breaking the law an acceptable everyday occurrence. Illegal acts are so commonplace that people often see the legal system as an ineffective joke, a development which has a strong impact on our young folks.

Drug abuse by a large number of our young people plays havoc within families. Parental caring, concern, and authority become increasingly meaningless to children as they become more involved in the illegal world of dope, a world of street games and street values and altered consciousness. What used to be exclusively the plague of the urban poor now haunts the middle and upper classes of urban, suburban, and small town America.

Phyllis recalls her teenage years and drug experimentation in New York City. When she was a teenager she smoked pot, tried cocaine, sniffed heroin, and occasionally drank, but there is a big difference between her drug use and what is happening today. Alcohol was not something she cared about, perhaps because it was frowned upon by her Jewish culture and she didn't like the alcohol high anyway. But she liked the feelings she got when she used pot and cocaine and if she were a kid today she feels that she'd abuse these chemicals. But Phyllis couldn't get drugs in high school. She got them from friends who were musicians who had connections in Spanish Harlem. On occasion she would be invited to parties where pot and drugs were given out. These were unusual events and she had to go out of her way to get and use them. They were not part of her normal life and their availability was limited and considered extraordinary.

The difference for kids today is enormous. Drugs are an everyday occurrence and easily available to every young person. Finding something to get high with is as easy as locating fast food. These chemicals are used for their own sake and for no other effect than the pleasure of getting high. Even the term "getting high" suggests the purpose of these experiences. We used to talk about exploring higher consciousness or altered states of reality, but "seeking" with drugs is not even mentioned today. The rush of immediate pleasure and gratification is the goal.

At one time drugs were part of "limit breaking" and the "new consciousness," but as the years have passed they have simply become part of the culture and like any product for sale, a market has been created and maintained. Teenagers are a major segment of that market.

There is no clear evidence or understanding as to which youth will get trapped by dope and its values and which youth won't. The argument that parents are the major factor makes no sense when we see so many families with one or two abusers and other children doing well. The problem and its solution are entangled in our culture's ambivalent stand on drugs and alcohol. Until we face the issue and resolve how we are going to handle drugs, young people will continue to act out our ambivalence.

Television, often blamed for our social problems, certainly has made a contribution. Young children are exposed to a myriad of influences and information, much of which may be inappropriate. Violence, often cited as a negative influence, is but one characteristic of current programs. Portraying policemen as boobs, politicians as rascals, and moonshiners as heroes, shows like "Dukes of Hazzard" provide a continuous challenge to our values and beliefs, an inundation that radio and movies never attained. Television all too often settles for cheap sensationalism and the economic exploitation of every age group, based on the belief that "what's good for General Motors is good for the country," a marketplace value that is not necessarily appropriate for family life.

Making commercial television the whipping boy for society's ills is unjust. Television reflects the culture as much as it shapes it and gives us only what we're willing to watch. But its net effect is to give parents much less control over their children's environment.

Television is part of the new technology. When we saw the astronauts walking on the moon, it was forever changed from green cheese to hard dusty matter. Out went the old fantasies and in came our fascination with rockets and computers. Our new technology has had its influence on family problems as well. Besides creating more chemicals to alter consciousness, like LSD, Valium, and Quaaludes, modern chemistry brings us "the pill." Birth control technology has reduced the risks of pregnancy associated with sexual intercourse and created a much more accepting climate for active sexuality.

When birth control pills first arrived on the American scene, parents who felt that sex before marriage is wrong found that the fear of pregnancy had been removed as a deterrent and as an argument against premarital intercourse. The new technology rendered that rationale obsolete. Parallel cultural developments encouraged parents to allow their children more choice and decision-making out of respect for their emerging personalities, and the overall effect on parents was a great deal of confusion, perceived by others as permissiveness.

For better or worse, the family is a dynamic social

organization that responds to the world around it. Each of us likes to think that we are unique. Millions of us, each being unique in our designer jeans and jogging shoes, eating health foods and playing with electronic games. Even those who resist such fads are subject to more subtle tugs of culture. Feminism, ecology, and other social issues influence our underlying thoughts and behaviors. We and our families are very much products of our times but we have difficulty acknowledging that fact when it comes to our family problems.

Like a contractor who has lost the blueprints, we are building our homes without knowing what comes next. It seems clear to us that psychological explanations from previous decades do not really help us deal with today's family problems. We should be willing to look further for explanations and solutions, and then develop a new set of plans.

Chapter 4

Parents Are People Too

The fact that parents are people and not automatons adds to life's richness. Some of us are great in crises and mediocre in everyday interactions. Some of us are terrific providers and terrible at giving physical affection. Others are aware and able to give emotional support but fall apart when it comes to helping with homework. Most of us do the best we can. It would be wonderful if we became parents and suddenly knew and could do everything. Whether parents are portrayed as omnipotent or helpless, malevolent or kind, they are, after all, only people.

"Parents are people too." The second of the TOUGH-LOVE Ten Beliefs may seem obvious but we have found that it helps parents to be reminded: not gods are we, but mortal beings struggling on the face of the earth. Amid that struggle we have a blessed event: our children.

The act of giving birth to or adopting a child identifies us as parents. As new parents we have hopes, dreams, and wishes for our children and for ourselves. As our infant grows through childhood to adolescence and adulthood, we experience changes. Changes which we recognized were possible but for which we had no way of preparing ourselves in advance. Changes like a marriage coming apart, a hyperactive child, deaths in the family, sickness, job layoffs, or just getting older. These changes often interfere with our hopes, dreams, wishes, and our best intentions. But having identified us as parents, our present culture would have us give up our human frailties and foibles and assume the powers of superbeings from the planet Krypton. The funny thing is that we too believed that we could cope with life's vicissitudes with relative ease.

When her mother died Phyllis was devastated. We had recently moved to Vermont, far from the urban environment that we experienced all our lives. With our young daughters we were struggling to make the adjustments to a new environment, a new job, and the new challenges of children entering school, all in the midst of the renovation of our new house, a story in itself.

We had lived near Phyllis's family during most of our marriage. The loss of her mother in this period of adjustment could not have come at a worse time, but life doesn't allow us to choose in such matters. As an only child Phyllis had a particularly close attachment to her mother and it was almost a year until her deep depression subsided. And David wasn't the greatest support to her, for he was preoccupied with the demands of his new career and rather intolerant of her pain and struggle.

Phyllis had trouble just getting out of bed in the morning. And her emotional trauma was exacerbated by guilt. She knew she wasn't giving to her children as she should but the demands of our new life and her own grief left her with limited energy.

Phyllis's guilt was to return and haunt her in later years. Although our other daughters seemed to weather those months with little difficulty, one daughter was deeply affected. She became very angry and withdrew from Phyllis while growing very attached to David. From time to time she would leave written messages around that said, "I hate my mother, I love my father."

When Phyllis had pulled herself together she tried to work out the estrangement with this daughter, but her efforts were fruitless. Although she apologized and explained, our daughter remained adamant. Not that there were obvious, continuous signs of resentment, but occasionally her behavior would reveal that she was still in the same place in her feelings toward her mom.

Not until eleven years later did the matter finally get resolved when Phyllis confronted her daughter, by then a young woman. "Look, when my mother died I was deeply saddened. I'm sorry I wasn't able to be there for you more than I was but I just wasn't. If you can't accept that it's just too bad, but you can't use it on me anymore."

She finally abandoned her guilt and demanded her daughter's acceptance, and the estrangement ended. Who knew that as parents we're not supposed to get depressed over our own mother's death? Sure it was a mistake to be bullied by her daughter for so long, but being a person as well as a parent, Phyllis has finally learned to accept her mistakes as well.

David remembers going to pick up one of his daughters from nursery school. When he arrived she was in the midst of hitting a smaller girl friend. Fearing that his daughter was becoming a bully, he smacked her on the behind and yelled, "Stop hitting." As he stood there he realized what a contradictory message he had just delivered and he started laughing, which was even more confusing to his daughter. The story simply illustrates how confusing and confused we can be as parents, no matter how much we reflect on our own actions.

Trying to be perfect makes us crazy. Accepting our own imperfection and doing the best that we can under existing circumstances keep us sane. If we can forgive our children for their mischief and mistakes, then we can also forgive ourselves. After all, parents are people too.

An expert's assessment in our local newspaper recently claimed that only 4 percent of our families really attain the open, honest, caring, and respectful relationship that *all* families are capable of. Upon first reading the article we felt bad and wished we had done a better job, then we suddenly regained consciousness from our guilty stupor. We realized that once again we were being presented with the idea of the perfect family. If only parents were more skilled, knowledgeable, and open, in short, more perfect, then our family would meet this expert's ideal.

The belief that the ideal is attainable can only lead to disappointment. For no matter how hard parents strive, the ideal is just some expert's neurotic dream. Consider the television program we saw the other night which emphasized the importance of "bonding" between mother and child at the moment of birth. According to the program babies should be delivered naturally, treated gently, and given to the mother as soon as possible. The scenes of mother and child were warm and tender. The doctor, still in his delivery room uniform, emanated competence and concern as he explained why this technique was the final word on childbirth. Imagine the feelings of all those parents out there in televisionland who had, like us, followed another birthing fad with our own children. Having now lived long enough we know that such information is just another nice idea getting a big play. But there is still that part of us that says, "See what a rotten start your kid had." We really feel for all the new parents and parents to be. These public "shoulds" and "oughts" encourage our feelings of guilt for not doing the best for our children.

Our culture currently bombards parents with so many different messages about the care and feeding of babies that we are fostering not only guilt, but confusion and self-doubt. "Shoulds" and "oughts" do not help parents, they only undermine their sense of worth. And for parents whose children are acting out, the feeling of failure is almost unbearable. When they first come to a TOUGHLOVE support group they are so burdened with guilt that they cannot think clearly. Just like them, we found ourselves searching for reasons for our daughters' outrageous behavior in our mistakes as parents. The fact that our daughters had something to do with the problem seemed minor compared to our own sense of responsibility, a state of mind strongly supported by our culture.

"How could you let it go so far? How could you let things get so out of hand?" the therapist asked Phyllis over the phone.

"I don't know, I don't know, but I'll do whatever you say to stop it and to help her," Phyllis replied.

Pause.

"Well, what do you think you should do?" responded the therapist.

Phyllis looks back on that telephone conversation with dismay. To this day she thinks: what were "it" and "things" and just how did it happen? How could she have explained what her life was like and what was going on? Her life wasn't one-dimensional. One kid was staying out past curfew, another was home with the flu, she was just starting a part-time job, and David was feeling overwhelmed and underpaid. The washing machine had just broken and so on. What did it take for the problem to get our full attention?

And she recalls issues and life changes in those years. She grew from a person who took care of others and expected others to take care of her to a person who was responsible for herself and her choices. She changed from a person who felt obligated to family and tied down to one that wanted her family without the resentment that obligation breeds. The trip from being someone who was responsible for others to a self-responsible person was not smooth, nor was she always fair to others, but it had to happen for her own survival and it was the sixties and seventies that made it both easier and harder or perhaps possible for it to happen at all.

For many years Phyllis was only a heart without a head and that became unbearable. Her own head needed to develop so she could be less dependent on her husband, the head. It is terrible to be all heart and emotion. There is no way to modify pain, fear, and loving. There is always the fear of falling into the abyss of feelings without being able to stop. She was always dependent on someone to stop her, to ground her and angry that she could not think, and so she had to develop her own head. The women's movement gave her permission to change and a way to define her troubles and her oppression.

She wanted to be a better role model for her daughters. She wanted them to know they could change, that they were people who could be mothers, not mothers who were trying to be people through mothering. If Phyllis was dependent on her motherhood for her identity, to be a person, then she was dependent for her life on her kids. In some ways what she wanted for her kids probably didn't and couldn't happen. She now thinks that people develop through roles they play and experiences they have, and it is not until later in life that a relatively autonomous self develops that can be interdependent and truly cooperative.

Phyllis hears the resentment when our daughter says to her, "You created the family you wanted." And when another says, "You were never consistent. Every time we moved I got depressed and still you wanted us to leave you alone, you didn't want to always be there." They are right and what they say is true. And she hears the yearning and entitlement in their voices and knows that they have struggles ahead, just as each one of us does.

Phyllis hears her kids when they say she had little empathy and yelled and blared, and it was that behavior that she fought to grow out of. It seems to her that she started with little self and had to develop. Our children seem to have an exaggerated sense of self, but they will have to fill in what's missing. Phyllis could see the world around her but not herself. Our children seem to see themselves and not the world. Neither is real. She is sorry for the harshness in their lives and is glad at the love in it. She feels like a puritan when she says she's glad for the struggle they will have to go through, a process she knows will affect their children also.

Every parent fails in some ways and perhaps it's a good thing. Parents can only teach what they know. Some of what they teach is inappropriate for the next generation, for things change very quickly. Most parents are strong in some areas and weak in others. Each generation's children need to learn new things so they can be of their own time, and each new person needs to develop that which will become their adult self. The goal is the balance of old and new.

How wonderful that we can now know and correct learning disabilities, spot epilepsy in its minor forms, recognize and compensate for a variety of problems. We have become very good at diagnosis, but not so good at helping people accept and deal with life in an imperfect world.

Now we have drugs and drug abuse. It seems to us that drugs tend to keep young people resentful, grudging infants. Some kids use drugs to avoid facing growing up and accepting that they are not the center of the universe, but part of it. The result is that the conflicts and pain of maturing are expressed in angry rage. This is a very new problem needing new solutions, one that we as parents have no way of immediately recognizing or correcting.

The problem has become part of a battle that is going on in our society. A battle that centers on children and how to show love and concern for them. The Moral Majority wants to make the world safe for kids by going back to old values, the legal community protects children by establishing laws against abuse, social workers protect them by becoming friends and allies, schools protect them by teaching them new information and by teaching parents parenting.

But our culture is so economically exploitative of children that it is difficult if not impossible to protect them fully. Advertisers bombard kids with commercials aimed at manipulating their tastes and their parents' buying decisions. Promoting junk food and jeans, tunes and toys, the airwaves saturate kids with commercial hype. Most recently television commercials have turned to the exploitation of adolescent and even pre-adolescent sexuality in selling products to buyers of all ages.

We expect parents to be omnipotent and omniscient and are disappointed because they are not. We cannot tell you how many times we have heard the phrase "Parents just don't care nowadays" from police, teachers, social workers, or others involved with unruly young people. The statement is particularly interesting when the police, teachers, social workers, and others are currently parents themselves.

We may have been stupid, misguided, helpless, stuck, angry, and inappropriate with our kids but we sure as hell *cared* about them. It is exactly the fact that folks care so much about their children and their role as parents that prevents them from taking some of the difficult stances that today's problem kids need.

How ironic that the search for the perfect parent persists while our culture busily undermines the confidence and authority of parents. Parenting courses try to provide blueprints for parents but also have the effect of undermining parents' confidence. There is always someone with yet another view who is kind enough to correct a wayward parent. We have come to rely on psychologists and therapists who constantly give us new ways to raise our children—it's like a psychological horn of plenty that buries parents with its wares, creating incompetence and helplessness. But the quest for the perfect parents pursues an illusion and we must accept the reality that, after all, parents are people too.

Chapter 5

Limited Resources

Phyllis used to wish she was a fountain of unending strength and that she could help her family with everything, solve problems, give guidance, and set people on the right road. She wanted to be Wonder Woman. It took her kids getting into real trouble to let her know she was a mere mortal. Phyllis, like most parents today, learned the hard way that her material and emotional resources are limited.

The belief that parents' material and emotional resources are limited is tough to accept in our hard-sell, "buy, buy, buy, be, be, be" culture. A television ad that clearly points this out is one in which an attractive woman opens a door and we see a bunch of kids in the middle of a pillow fight, bedding all over the place, and everything in a mess. The woman hollers and tells the kids to be quiet and stop their fighting. The children stare at her in utter amazement. She closes the door, holds her head, and mutters, "If it wasn't for this headache." After she takes two aspirin, the room is clean and orderly and the commercial closes with a happy "milk and cookies for all" note.

The message is clear. If only Mom wouldn't have

something internally wrong with her the family would be O.K. And the cure for Mom's problem is the ingestion of some magic pill which is so wonderful that it even transforms her kids. "So remember, parents, if your kids are being rowdy it's probably because there is something wrong with you. After all, good parents don't let a little thing like a headache stop them. You have unlimited resources, some as close as your medicine cabinet, to cope with your problems."

An example of how we personally struggled with accepting our limited resources as parents was what we refer to as our "horse fiasco." When we lived in the Virgin Islands each of our kids had a horse of her own. Horses were cheap to buy and even cheaper to maintain. The horses ate the abundant tropical grass and needed grain occasionally and shoeing every once in a while. Of course we had to have dogs too, a Lassie and a Rin Tin Tin.

Moving to Pennsylvania meant leaving the horses but we brought our two large faithful canine companions with us. It was difficult finding a place to live for three children, two dogs, and us. It meant paying more rent but our kids' happiness was at stake. Despite the sacrifice our children were unhappy about the move anyway and complained constantly about not having a horse.

Finally we gave in. We bought a horse, rented a stable, worked out a transportation schedule, and we asked our kids to help out by doing necessary chores around the house. The expense, the energy, and the time involved was more than we could manage and we had to get rid of the horse at a considerable loss of money. Our kids responded with angry behavior even though they had never kept their part of the bargain.

We wish we could say that we learned from the

experience, but we didn't. We were trying to make things nice for our children. We hoped to maintain a happy, healthy interest for our kids and allow them to see what good parents we really were. The plan backfired because our fantasy did not match the reality of our limited resources. And to top everything off, one of the dogs ran away.

We know many parents who want the best possible life for their children and, like we did, get caught up in being super parents. Taking kids for dancing lessons, Little League, music, wrestling, gymnastics, all so their kids can be happy All-American achievers. Parents make these efforts, arrange schedules, root at games, and then they are accused of living vicariously through their children and putting excessive pressure on them. If a parent doesn't do all those things, they're perceived as uncaring and if they do, they're seen as hurtful.

Children play a role in this phenomenon. Most kids want to keep up with others and even excel. They want to be on the team, get an A, and be in the best group. Competition fuels the fires that consume our limited material and emotional resources.

When parents have trouble with their kids people often fail to recognize a parent's limited resources, as this anecdote will illustrate. When Paula first came to the TOUGHLOVE group she seemed shocked by the stories of drugs, drunkenness, and violence many of the parents told. "I think maybe I don't belong here," she exclaimed. "My son's just skipping school."

Johnny, her eleven-year-old, had begun staying home from school and watching television every day, coming and going as he pleased. Paula, a single parent since her husband's death two years before, worked full-time and had difficulty trying to keep Johnny in school. He was utterly defiant, so she and Johnny had been going to counseling at the recommendation of his school. She was troubled by the cost but she wanted to help her son in any way she could.

Following traditional psychological theories, the counselor focused on Johnny's need to express and talk about the grief, anger, and guilt associated with his father's death in order to achieve acceptance of that traumatic event. When he completed this process, the counselor assured Paula, Johnny's destructive behavior would cease. He advised Paula to be tolerant of the process and communicate more with Johnny, sharing memories of her husband and urging the boy to do the same.

In the meantime Paula saw that Johnny's behavior was getting worse so she decided to attend a meeting of the local TOUGHLOVE parent/community support group. Experienced group members asked Paula how she reacted to Johnny when she discovered that he had left school after she had dropped him off. She stated that her usual reaction was to cry and plead with him. The parents listened carefully. Since Paula seemed very timid about taking any immediate steps the parents simply urged her to read some of the TOUGHLOVE materials and come back to the next meeting. Another woman in the group offered to call her during the week to see how she was doing.

By the next meeting Paula had several more upsetting incidents with Johnny and felt she had to take some action. When she met with the counselor he encouraged her to be patient but at the TOUGHLOVE meeting she broke into tears and declared that she couldn't stand it anymore. Her boss was complaining about her absentmindedness at work, she wasn't sleeping well, and she was feeling exhausted.

The other parents in the group helped her formulate a plan, but checked Paula's resolve by asking several times if she was sure she was ready to take such action. She insisted that she was.

The next evening two sets of parents came to Paula's home to talk with Johnny. They told him that he must go to school and stay there the next day and every day thereafter, no matter how unhappy he was. The two fathers agreed to call Johnny every night to see how he was doing and Paula agreed to call the Big Brother organization for him.

Paula reported at the next meeting that Johnny seemed frightened by the other parents coming into his home but that he had not missed a day of school since. He was now on the waiting list for a Big Brother and he accepted the two fathers calling him. In fact he seemed to look forward to their calls.

The story of Paula and Johnny highlights other reasons for the third of the Ten Beliefs, that "Parents' material and emotional resources are limited." Although the counselor acknowledged Paula's own grief at her husband's death, somehow he could excuse the boy's self-destructive behavior and ask Paula to endure while Johnny resolved his grief. Paula was perceived as an omnipotent being who did not need support to manage her own grief but had the emotional resources to cope with the extensive demands now being made on her. Even though he charged a reduced fee in light of her financial situation, the therapist also assumed that she had the material resources to pay counseling fees for a long time.

It's very important to notice that our culture expects parents to tough it out and not let death affect their behavior toward their children, while a child's manipulative, power-playing behavior will be tolerated because of the psychological difficulties in dealing with death. Certainly we can expect an adult's maturity to make a difference in his or her coping skills, but the disparity of expectations is unreasonable.

We cannot assume that parents' resources are unlimited. For that assumption actually encourages destructive young people to continue their behavior while demanding patient acquiescence from adults. Parents have both the right and the need to say, "This is my limit. I've had enough. I need something from you now."

The Santa Claus syndrome demonstrates our own unrealistic demands on ourselves. We stretch our budgets like rubber bands to get our children presents. Even when our children are misbehaving we somehow put aside our anger and disappointment for the Christmas season and spend a lot of money on our undeserving and unappreciative youngsters.

During one of our daughters' druggie days we went out shopping for a new winter coat for her. She must have tried on a hundred coats but none of them pleased her. Then she tried on a very expensive suede coat. It was beautiful and she looked great in it. The price was a small fortune relative to our funds. Despite the fact that she had been a nasty shrew in recent months we decided to take the plunge. Maybe she would appreciate us more and behave better. After all, it was a good coat and would last a couple of years. Within one week the coat was muddy and bedraggled, a victim of her stoned indifference.

We knew that we couldn't buy love but we hoped

that this sacrifice would make a difference. We hoped she would see in this luxury purchase the caring that she didn't seem to recognize in other ways.

Our material resources are limited and young people need to understand that. Designer jeans are not a fundamental right or a necessity, but we often spend the bucks without demanding anything in return. And by not demanding anything in return we actually rob our children of opportunities to learn necessary responsibility.

Perhaps unruly children don't appreciate us because we don't appreciate ourselves. When we give away our love for free we devalue its worth. Something for nothing is valued as nothing. Recently one of our daughters told us, "The more you gave us, the more I took for granted my right to have these things. When what I wanted or wished for wasn't given I felt deprived and thought you were being mean and punishing."

We also have to respect our own emotional limits. When the culture is telling us to be hip, to accept new moral values about sex or drugs, we have to ask ourselves if we can tolerate the emotional consequences of denying our own feelings. If we feel O.K. with the issue, then fine. For instance, some TOUGHLOVE parents smoke marijuana themselves and have set limits for their cooperative teenagers which include occasional social use of pot. We do not prescribe this or any other particular set of values and if you can live with that situation, that's up to you. But if you feel you can't, then pay attention to your own emotional limits and respect your right to have them and impose them on your children until they are of age and responsible to decide for themselves.

In a society that is obsessed with children and their

needs, as we seem to be, we have created a fundamental imbalance in families. Surely children are important and need to be loved and sometimes indulged. But so do adults. Parents have feelings and needs that require attention from their children.

One of our daughters consistently failed to remember Phyllis's birthday, and Phyllis tends to be pretty extravagant with presents. She would get our daughter expensive gifts without any reciprocation. That is, until she recognized her own emotional needs and her right to feel appreciated. On our daughter's next birthday Phyllis gave her a card and burst out laughing. When asked why she felt good about not giving her daughter a present, Phyllis said that she felt free. It was liberating to finally give what she had been getting. Our daughter got the message and she's been pretty good about our need to be recognized and appreciated. Anyway, she has not missed Phyllis's birthday ever since.

Our own experience since our most troubled days has taught us that our children respect us more now that we make demands on them. Why we waited so long to do so is a difficult question to answer but we urge those parents who are stuck in the same place we were to recognize their own limits and act accordingly.

Chapter 6

Kids Are Not Equal

The most difficult of the TOUGHLOVE Ten Beliefs for many people to accept, at least among those who attend our weekend workshops, is the fourth, which states, "Parents and kids are not equal." People seem to get confused with the assertion in the American Declaration of Independence, "that all men are created equal, that they are endowed by their Creator with certain unalienable Rights, that among these are Life, Liberty and the pursuit of Happiness."

Far be it from us to challenge the Declaration of Independence, but we're reasonably certain that the Founding Fathers would agree with us. Every state and provincial government in the United States and Canada defines an age of majority, the age when young people assume the legal rights of citizens. Until then they are clearly in the care of their parents or legal guardians and by no means are they equal before the law.

Despite that legal definition people still get hung up in other kinds of equality. The confusion in our culture is illustrated by a television commercial which shows two small children at a table waiting as their father is readying breakfast in the background. The two cherubs begin banging on the table like prisoners in the old Cagney movies and chanting in nagging tones, "We want Thomas', we want Thomas'." Dad delivers the goods with a smile that shows his joy at pleasing his tormentors. The kids finish eating and Dad comments that it's now their turn to clean up. The kids' response is a Bronx cheer.

It's obvious that in terms of equality, the children in this family are "more equal" than Dad. Although the commercial's intended effect is cute and funny, the destructive young people with whom we deal in this book express this attitude in ways that are not cute or funny. Unruly children treat parents as objects to be manipulated for their pleasure, an infantile position that they support by arguments based on their being equal. "You drink, so why can't I smoke dope?" Or, "You stay out late, so why can't I?" When we attempt to refute these arguments with reason and logic we have really already lost because they are not interested in dialogue, just in getting what they want. Fairness, trust, honesty, openness, and communication or any similar values we hold set us up for manipulation with this kind of kid, especially if he or she is someone we love.

The argument that people should be "reasonable" with their children is a very fine ideal indeed and easily achieved with children who are so inclined. But for the kind of young people we're dealing with reasonableness is a one-way street, in their favor.

At our TOUGHLOVE Weekend Workshops, which we discuss in Chapter 14, this confusion about equality is demonstrated in a little role play in which one of us acts the part of an unreasonable child while a parent or professional attending the workshop volunteers to play the reasonable parent. It goes something like this.

"I will not permit you to smoke marijuana."

"Listen, Dad, you relax with a cocktail when you get home. I just want to relax with a little grass."

"Well, marijuana is illegal."

"Oh, come on, Dad. Having under an ounce is only a misdemeanor and anyway everyone does it. Even the cops don't care. Besides, when you let me have wine at dinner, that's illegal."

The argument then swirls around in a multitude of directions, all of them missing the essential point that children and their parents are not equal. Parents do not need to win arguments to make their point. They have the responsibility for the children in their household and they have the authority to decide what is appropriate for those children, within certain bounds of law and tradition.

One family we know of which is *not* having troubles with its children has adopted a position that is based simply on parental authority. The father, who smokes marijuana occasionally, was discovered by his high school-age daughter. When she challenged him with "How come you can smoke grass and I can't?" his response was simple: "Because I have a double standard and I say you can't." In this family the parents clearly assert the inequality of their relationship with their children in the parents' favor.

The point we are making should not be clouded by the reader's feelings about the legality or appropriateness of the father smoking marijuana. The point is that parents do have double standards in regard to their own behavior and that of their children, particularly as it relates to things like alcohol or staying out late. Adults are responsible for themselves and their children are not.

Parents and children have different roles in a family. Parents guide and protect and their children grow and mature. Parents, by virtue of their life experience, are assumed to have better judgment than their children. Although that may not always be the case, it's a reasonably good bet. Therefore parents make decisions about how to protect their children from whatever they think is harmful. That determination may vary from family to family, but we can't think of a better system for developing healthy children. It's not only a time-honored tradition for parents to be in charge, but the family needs the maturity of adult leadership.

In another family we know the parents recently struggled with the equality issue when their eight-year-old son was writing a letter to his former third grade class. Usually he is very proud of his writing and wants to read his letters out loud to his parents before he sends them. On this particular occasion when his mom asked him how his letter was going, he smiled strangely and said that it was already sealed. She had a funny feeling that the letter was inappropriate and asked him to let her read it.

"I don't read your letters," he said and she backed off.

Moments later she discussed the matter with Dad and he pointed out that she was getting herself confused about her son's rights.

"You're his parent and if you have a feeling that the letter is not appropriate then you have the right to intervene. So what if he doesn't read your letters. You're in charge."

Mom went back to her son and demanded the letter. He blushed and immediately began writing a new one while she read the first one. He knew the letter made nasty statements about other children and would have been very embarrassing and hurtful to some of his old friends if it were read by the class. He made no further objections. Later the eight-year-old told his mom that he was glad she had intervened and that he would have been sorry about mailing the letter.

We are not suggesting that children have no privacy or that parents should indiscriminately impose their will at every turn. But parents follow their instincts and intelligence as best they can and when they feel they must, they have both the right and the obligation to intervene in their child's life. The relationship between parents and their children is quite different from the relationship between government and its citizens as defined in the Bill of Rights.

We followed the style of the democratic family during the sixties. When you have more than two kids you're always outvoted—not a situation for a parent to get into.

The heart of the equality issue does not rest on legality. For instance, parents whose young adult children are living with them still have the right to set standards in their household even though these children have reached the age of majority. When parents are earning the money, paying the rent or mortgage, buying the groceries, taking the responsibility for keeping the household running smoothly, and providing emotional support as well, a child has no right to claim authority over anything, not even his or her "own" room. In truth it's not his or her room, it's the parents' room. Privacy is a privilege that grows out of cooperation.

Young people are in a dependent situation when they're living at home. They may not like to admit it, but without their parents' support they could not manage their lives. Those teenagers who are cooperative recognize and accept their dependency on their parents and family.

Sometimes a child with a disability—genetic, from an accident, or imaginary—manages to achieve disproportionate power in a family. He or she is given such help, concern, and attention that instead of being in the presumed inferior position because of disability the child has achieved dominance.

We knew a family that had gone to counseling because their thirteen-year-old daughter, Mary, felt "bad" about herself, was disrespectful, and fought constantly with her younger siblings. After two years of building her ego with dance lessons, special piano lessons, weekly counseling sessions, and lots of praise, all at the advice of the family counselor, Mary acted as though she ran the family and in truth she did, for the attention in the family was always focused on her. She was more than equal, she was the queen bee and the rest of the family members were drones. Now this TOUGHLOVE family struggles with the difficult steps necessary to correct the situation, which include paying less attention to Mary and more to her siblings.

Equality is a tough issue in our culture. Many groups of people have forced us to examine how our prejudices have created inequalities, and rightly so. But young people are in the process of achieving equality and they must understand that their parents' fairness, trust, reasonableness, and other "goodies" are not unalienable rights but must be earned and maintained by their own demonstrated responsibility. As parents we can accept our responsibility of preserving appropriate double standards and recognizing that "Parents and kids are *not* equal."

Chapter 7

Blame

"Have you hugged your kid today?" The question is asked by a bumper sticker on the car in front of you or by a public service message on your television screen. Assuming that the car's driver and the television station's programming manager are motivated by altruism, then they are simply trying to heighten other people's awareness of the needs of children and encourage parents to be loving and caring.

On the other hand, the statement "Have you hugged your kid today?" is based on the underlying assumption that many parents don't and that's why we're having so much trouble with kids today. This blaming message offers an extremely simplistic solution for a very complex problem.

But that's the way it is with blame. Blaming allows us to focus our anger and in our most sanctimonious and righteous manner we can vent our spleen and walk away feeling satisfied.

Blame has become the favorite American pastime. The problem of unruly young people is most often blamed on uncaring parents. Parents and other people also blame the teachers who don't maintain discipline in

schools, the police who don't enforce the laws, the
judges who let criminals off the hook, the psychiatrists
who keep people coming back for expensive sessions,
the pushers who seduce young people into the world of
drugs, the politicians who are all taking bribes, the
teenager's peer group which leads the innocent child
astray, unhealthy sugar-laden food which causes hyper-
activity, the feminist movement which pushes moms
out of the home, television and movies which encourage sex and violence, divorce, lack of religion, children's
rights, and on and on.

Blame can be a lot of fun and very creative. It keeps
us busy with the illusion of knowing the cause of
something so we really don't have to accomplish anything productive. Focusing on an illusion is a surefire
way not to solve the problem.

As family therapists we were also very good at blame.
Implicit in our method was blame for parents. Of
course we never said that we were blaming parents, but
that's exactly what we did. We sincerely hope our
earliest clients survived us, but if it's any consolation to
them we found ourselves in their shoes and the change
of role helped us realize what we had been doing.

Most families, like ours, go to family therapy in
desperation, reaching out for help. We had just moved
to Lansdale, Pennsylvania, from the Virgin Islands.
This was our third move in four years and we were
trying to start new jobs, make a home, and get our
family settled. With all this going on we were somewhat oblivious to the difficulties our children were
experiencing, particularly our thirteen-year-old daughter.
We felt a vague discomfort about her behavior at home
and the less than desirable friends she was making. She
talked occasionally about her troubles at school, how

the school work was different and how the teachers and
other students made it difficult for newcomers. We
shared her negative feelings about the schools, having
been influenced by the antiauthority notions of the
sixties, and we reinforced her rebellious attitude with
our sympathy.

Eventually the school called us to come in for a
meeting about her behavior and we went, reluctantly
and resentfully. We had to take off from work, make
different travel arrangements, and go back into that
old-fashioned institution with bells, rows of desks, and
chalkboards. We felt the long-forgotten feeling of being
in trouble and having to go to the principal's office and
the new feeling of shame and embarrassment as parents
who had to go to school because of our child. None of
our own parents ever had to go to school for us and we
knew this identified us as "bad parents."

David remembers feeling very ambivalent. On one
hand he accepted that everything was our fault and that
we were among a small number of parents who had this
kind of experience. On the other hand he thought the
school had been very rigid and unsupportive to our
daughter as a recent arrival. Of course he based that on
what she had told him and he was not yet aware of how
deceptive and manipulative she could be.

We were not receptive to the school people. We
blamed them and they blamed us. In retrospect, neither
we nor the school folks were very honest with each
other. We didn't level with them about our daughter
and they didn't level with us about the large number of
kids in the school who were acting just like ours. We
thought our daughter was reacting to the difficulties of
fitting into a new school environment. Had we known
how commonplace her behavior was we would have felt

much less defensive. On the school folks' part, they were getting blamed by the public for Johnny's failure to read and attacked as medieval institutions. They felt defensive also. All in all, it was a no-win situation for everyone.

Things cooled down for a while, at least as far as we knew, until one night we were roused from our complacency by a telephone call from the local hospital. Our daughter, who had gone out to a school dance, had been in an auto accident and was now in the hospital emergency room. She had a broken nose but was otherwise all right. When we went to pick her up she was lying quietly on a cot in a room divided by white canvas curtains. Our daughter seemed unclear about what had happened except that somehow the brakes had failed. Our concern and curiosity were aroused and we looked around to see who else had been in the accident. Then we realized that she had been with a young woman whom we had forbidden her to see and two sleazy-looking fellows. We were so frightened and upset by her disregard for our wishes and her choice of friends that we decided to seek family therapy.

Philadelphia, being one of the most creative centers for family therapy, offered us quite a selection. As therapists ourselves we were knowledgeable about the alternatives. We chose a place with an excellent reputation and put ourselves in our therapists' hands. They used inter-generational theory, which meant that we, as parents, had unresolved issues with our own parents that were leading to difficulties with our children. We had gone to counseling before and worked on feelings and thoughts about our parents so that the early sessions seemed very redundant. When we commented on this and pointed out how rudely our children were behaving in the sessions, slouching in their chairs with their feet on the table, pretending to sleep, we were told, "Leave them alone, they are only children."

The sessions continued on about our families of origin. From these sessions we learned to be more compassionate and accepting toward the life choices our parents made, but received little help with our children's behavior, which is why we went there in the first place.

The real message was coming through loud and clear. Because we had unresolved feelings about our parents it was our fault that our daughter was having trouble. Guilt and blame were exactly what we didn't need and we began to blame each other, get angry, and fight, a fact that probably led our therapists to feel they were making progress. Blame, shame, and guilt accumulated while our daughter's behavior became worse. We finally left, seeking other help.

We tried several therapists and a psychiatrist. Each attempt left us feeling a little more helpless and inadequate and a little more blamed. We tried home tutoring, private school, and finally allowed our daughter to quit school and get a job. She worked as a waitress in a local hotel restaurant and seemed to be settling down once again. She was seeing a psychiatrist who had supported this change and we breathed a sigh of relief.

Our daughter needed working papers and our permission to leave school. The school insisted that we come in personally to sign the necessary forms and we were lectured about dooming our child to failure by not forcing her to continue her education. A school official who verified that departing students were actually employed made a point of telling our daughter each time he saw her what awful parents we were. We felt that no matter what solutions we tried someone was going to blame us for the problem.

When we were studying, practicing, and training others in family counseling, we were intrigued by the patterns in a family's history, the family's myths, the different roles family members played, the birth order of children, and the effects of all these factors on the problem which brought the family into therapy. We were so pleased with ourselves when we spotted and helped correct faulty communication between family members. We thought we were so smart when the "real meaning" behind nonverbal gestures and behaviors became clear. And we still feel there is much truth to many of the creative theories about how families function. But theory is abstract and people are not. Theories may help us to understand the framework of what is happening, but what good is a method of working with the client that doesn't make sense to the client?

The hard test of theory is whether it helps solve the problem that is bothering the client right now, not some abstract problem that the counselor sees through the lens of his or her pet theory. People suffering with a problem are not intellectual exercises. They are usually people with a pressing problem and they want real concrete help. When we went to therapy our self-image was at an all-time low and our guilt and anxiety were sky-high. We could not understand what the therapist was doing. We wanted guidance, support, and direction to help us manage our home and our kids. But what we got was blame.

Working out the issues we had with our parents might have been an interesting exercise but not while our children were behaving horribly. Although the therapeutic theory was supposed to help resolve our problems in the long run, in the short run we didn't know what to do.

We learned a lot from that experience. We learned how our clients feel. We learned that solving the problem in the present is all-important and that as helpers to people we must explain the problem in terms that our clients can clearly understand. We recognized that people can learn new behaviors and can look back at their pasts in different ways. We learned that support for change is necessary and we had better be able to give clear directions to solve the problem, although that doesn't mean that every solution is a happy one. But most significantly we learned the futility of blame.

The way in which we therapists blame is by thinking and acting as if the children in the family are victims of their parents' anomalies. As long as parents are accepting the rap for their offsprings' behavior their children can't change.

We are now aware of the power of "victims." When an unruly youth says to us, "My mother hated me, my father never paid attention to me, my uncle exposed himself to me," regardless of whether the accusations are true or not, first we show some empathy and then we ask the question, "And how do you get revenge?"

Whether there are reasons for destructive behavior or not, each young person makes choices and he or she has the power to choose behaviors that will make life go better. Putting the responsibility for behavior on external forces and perceiving the young person as a helpless victim is both condescending and unproductive. When therapists, counselors, psychologists, or psychiatrists do that, they become part of the problem.

The psychological victim concept has become so pervasive in our culture that it's part of the problem on a societal scale. Perhaps we can best sum up the dynamics of blame by presenting a construct that we adapted from transactional analysis. It's called the blame game.

The blame game has three roles for players. As few as two people can play at a time. The roles are victim, persecutor, and rescuer. The victim is a poor, unjustly accused person, the persecutor is the one who is unjustly accusing the victim, and the rescuer saves the poor, unjustly accused person. In this way the rescuer will surely be appreciated by the victim.

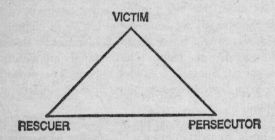

Betty hears her daughter coming up the steps and looks at the clock on her dresser. It's only nine o'clock and June usually doesn't get home until eleven.

"June, how come you're home from work so early?"

Her daughter comes into her bedroom, her face downcast.

"Oh, what's the matter, dear? Did something happen?"

"Yeah, but I don't want to talk about it."

Betty gets up and puts her arms around her daughter.

"It's always best to talk about things that are bothering you. What happened? Did you have trouble with Smitty again?"

"Yeah."

"Well, I know how bitchy some bosses can get. Tell me what happened."

June has her mom pretty well set for the news.

"Well, Smitty was a real grouch tonight. We were super busy and he was complaining about how we stack the dirty dishes. Some fell over and he blamed me. It could have been anyone, but he blamed me."

Betty listened with sympathy. It wasn't every day she got the chance to be her daughter's rescuer. Usually she was her persecutor. Her daughter, of course, was always the victim.

"Anyhow, I've had it up to here. I told him to get off my back. I mean I didn't curse or anything. Well hardly. But with some people you can't even get a little angry. He told me to leave."

"Oh my. Well, at least you got paid yesterday. You can make your car payment that's due and you'll still get a few days' pay that he owes you now to hold you until you get another job."

June delivers the final blow.

"I don't have the money for the car payment."

Betty feels anger, then desperation. Suddenly Smitty drops from her mind as persecutor and her daughter takes his place. She feels like the victim.

"How could you do this to me? You promised when you quit school that if I cosigned for the car you'd never miss a payment. This is the third one. I just don't have the money. I'm a single parent and it's tough enough without paying for your car."

"Look, Mom. I just lost my job and all you can do is bitch about yourself. To hell with you."

June storms out of the room and out of the house, stopping briefly in her room for the hat she bought yesterday. She'll party with her friends, now that she's got the news off her chest and Mom back in the persecutor role where she belongs.

As the reader can see, the roles of victim, persecutor, and rescuer are not permanently assigned. They are very much "in the eyes of the beholder." But the young people with whom TOUGHLOVE deals almost always perceive themselves as victims, with their parents as persecutors, while counselors and other professional helpers often fill the rescuer slots.

There is only one way to get out of these roles and that's to stop playing the game. Accepting blame or putting blame on others keeps the game going. Asking young people, even small children, to accept the responsibility for their own actions is the way to avoid making them into victims. But the blame game is such a habit and the dynamics so familiar that we all have trouble backing off from it.

Consider the difficulty that our associates, Susan and Ted Wachtel, had with their own son, Josh, just last year. They both know all about the blame game and its roles and dynamics, having presented the game as trainers many times. Still they found themselves being players in their own family.

Josh, then in fourth grade, came home from elementary school and told his parents that he was in trouble for not having done his book reports.

"How many do you have to get done?"

"Seven."

"You mean you haven't done your book reports for seven weeks? How could your teacher let it go on for so long?"

The teacher is now the persecutor, Josh the victim.

Notice how someone else is taking the rap for Josh's irresponsibility.

"When do you have to have them done?"

"Well, I have to stay after school every day until they are finished."

Ted and Susan looked at each other. They just became the victims, with their son and his teacher being persecutors.

"You mean we have to pick you up after school until your book reports are done?" (Not really, for the school was within walking distance, but the district provided bus transportation.)

Josh looked sheepishly at the floor.

"I can't believe the teacher let these reports drag on like this. Seven weeks. Why can't she check on them more often?"

Josh's parents continued to play the game until dinner, when suddenly simultaneous recognition occurred. They looked at each other, then turned to their son and stopped playing the game.

"Josh, we're not coming to pick you up after school. After dinner we're going to work out a route for you to walk home which seems the safest and you're just going to have to get your book reports done. As far as we're concerned the problem is yours and you have to take care of it."

The game was over because the players backed out.

If two parents who train others in the blame game still get caught in it, one might ask how we expect other parents, especially single parents like Betty, to get out of the game by themselves. We don't. That's why we have developed the concept of TOUGHLOVE parent/community support groups. (See Chapter 14.) Let's go back to Betty's situation, just after June has stormed out of the house, and assume that Betty has been attending weekly sessions of a TOUGHLOVE group in her community. She phones a group member.

"Hello, Rachel. This is Betty. I'm in your TOUGH-LOVE group."

"Oh hi, Betty. You sat next to me last week, right?"

"Yes, that's me. I'm sorry to bother you but I just had a fight with my daughter and I'm really upset. Can you talk for a little while?"

"Of course."

Betty relates the incident to Rachel. Rachel listens and recognizes the blame game roles, which she and her husband get stuck in all the time. But somehow it's easier to see them in somebody else's family.

"Betty, I'm really glad you called. Do you want to come over for coffee and maybe you and my husband and I can come up with some ideas for how to deal with this situation?"

Rachel already had some idea of how to help Betty. Over coffee she and her husband relate a similar story about how they kept helping their son make his fine payments imposed by the court. They blamed the arresting officer, the judge, sometimes their son and always felt like persecuted victims. Until they decided to stop blaming and let their son take responsibility for the situation he created.

"But if she loses the car then I'll have to drive her to work," frets Betty.

Rachel understands her dilemma and tries to persuade her.

"First of all, she hasn't lost the car yet. Secondly, you don't have to drive her if she does. She has friends. There are taxi-cabs. Whatever."

Rachel's husband, Bob, intervenes.

"Rachel, I think we're trying to convince Betty of something that she's not ready to do yet."

Rachel nods and Bob continues.

"Betty, why don't you just think about the idea for now. When you come to the TOUGHLOVE meeting in two days you can bring up the situation again and discuss it with others. In the meantime feel free to call us again."

Betty seems more relaxed. The decision to get out of the game is not an easy one, but with support from other parents she is likely to make the move eventually.

Blame is the prevailing attitude among many professionals in the courts and social services as well. A young person's outrageous behavior brings him or her to the attention of these people but the "victim" theories divert the focus from the youth to the "causes" of his or her behavior.

We hate to tell you how many times families have gone to mental health workers, caseworkers, probation officers, or others and have been asked to let the worker "get to know them and then judge for themselves." This happens as the family bounces from one agency to another, as their child's behavior eventually becomes a legal issue and they end up in the courts.

The professional says that he or she needs time to win the *kid's* confidence. What about the parents' confidence? What about parents' assertions concerning what's been happening? The parents say that the kid is a druggie and has been robbing them blind, but often they are not believed because at the root of the professional's thinking is, all too frequently, the feeling that it's the parents' fault.

We know of situations where the family has gone

through this process a half dozen times as each new professional starts over. Instead of confronting the kid's behavior, regardless of why he or she is acting horribly, they first have to "understand" the situation and get to know the kid. No wonder many kids perceive adults as suckers whom they can manipulate. Sure, some parents are horrible and abusive, and that will come out, but in the meantime that does not give their offspring license to abuse others. Sure many kids need to sort out their feelings with the help of professionals, but why should they bother if we excuse their behavior?

Parents blame themselves as much as others do. They are products of their culture and they accept its patterns and practices. Feeling guilty is the result of self-blame which keeps parents from taking effective action in dealing with their kid.

Phyllis remembers the evening she was sitting in the bathtub filled with bubbles. She was just relaxing when her fourteen-year-old daughter came in to talk. She sat down on the floor and casually said, "Susan stayed out all night last week and this girl in school ran away a week ago. What would you do if I did that?" Phyllis replied, "Well, I would be really upset and I'd wonder why you'd want to do that." Our daughter continued, "Would you call the police?" "I haven't thought of what I'd do. No, I don't think I'd call the police, but why do you ask? Are you unhappy?" She shook her head. "No, just curious. No reason." And she left the room. Phyllis felt a little funny, anxious feeling but dismissed it.

A week or so later our daughter stayed out all night. We worried, paced the floor, and gave her until morning before we would call the police. After we got to work we called home and she'd returned. We decided to show our disapproval in a different way. Instead of the usual lecture we simply asked her never to do that again. Unfortunately she interpreted our reaction as not caring about her.

Phyllis now sees the inept way she handled the original situation with her daughter. When she first mentioned the idea of staying out all night, Phyllis didn't say to herself, "What's going on with her?" She didn't think it through nor did she get back to her. Now we advise parents to say that staying out is not permissible and that they *will* call the police. If the kid still does it, we urge them to get a third party to help talk to the kid when he or she gets back, especially if it's the first time.

As for herself, Phyllis felt horrible and guilty for being so insensitive, for not paying attention to her initial uneasiness with the situation. But her guilt did absolutely nothing to help the situation. Self-blame, like other kinds of blame, is useless in solving the problem. Everybody makes mistakes, so what's the point of beating yourself up over your blunders.

Sure, parents have a part in the problem and have made mistakes. But they need to make changes, not dwell in the past. Our experience with parents is that they recognize everything they think they did wrong with their children and then some. That's why they have so much trouble asking their kids to accept the consequences of their behavior.

There is an interesting assumption made by our critics in the psychiatric and psychological communities that TOUGHLOVE parents have not raised their children with structure or demands and suddenly they are imposing new rules and requirements. Not so. Most TOUGHLOVE parents did have effective discipline when their kids were younger, but find that in adolescence they are faced with a defiance that is beyond their previous experience and they don't know how to handle it.

When the old guidelines that parents think they have set begin to fail the parents are at a loss. The youngster begins to control and manipulate his or her parents by acting in unexpected ways for which there are no handy cultural solutions. How many parents know how to deal with a druggie? What do you do when you send your daughter to her room and she jumps out the window? Which disciplinary method do you use when your son says "fuck you" or beats you up? We're not talking about conventional child-rearing problems, we're talking about crises.

We hear a lot about parents' responsibility when a young person gets in trouble but we can't remember anyone seeing a kid do well and saying, "Gee, look how responsible these parents have been." The word responsibility is usually used when we blame or censure parents, not for praise.

Parents are treated like sinners and are asked by counselors and therapists to confess so they can be given absolution. This process is supposed to help children confess their own misdeeds and change their behavior. It sounds good but it doesn't work. With the kinds of families in our experience, the parents accept and admit their shortcomings and the children then use the information to stay the same. They say, "How can I change? Look how *you fucked me up*."

Finding out whose fault the problem is may seem like a good idea assuming that the culpable person knows how to fix what's wrong or the faultfinder can guide the person to the appropriate correction. But we have the feeling that most often responsibility is assigned to a person so that we can shake our finger at them and leave the situation for someone else to clean up.

A TOUGHLOVE parent we know was asked to speak to a local mental health clinic's staff about TOUGHLOVE and its effects on her life and family. Eventually the discussion came around to the idea of prevention and one counselor said, "You know, over half the kids at school are really in trouble, especially with drugs. The question is what are families who are producing good kids doing right?" The parent turned to the questioner and said that she wondered which category she would fit in, since her one kid was in trouble and the other two were on the honor roll and excelled in school sports. Was her family doing things right or wrong? The questioner faded back into the audience.

Calling parents irresponsible only brings up guilt, anger, and self-pity. We feel that it's much more accurate to say that parents have been "irresponsive." They have not responded appropriately to their children's behavior.

TOUGHLOVE is interested in helping parents, schools, police, probation officers, social workers, counselors, therapists, and anyone who has to deal with negative adolescent behavior learn to be *correctively responsive* to the problem. We can all sit around and blame each other or we can all cooperate and accomplish something. We are confident that the methods we have developed will work and that gradually communities throughout North America will recognize the fifth of the Ten Beliefs, "Blaming keeps people helpless." As long as our culture maintains its blaming stance we will be plagued by the outrageous behavior of the "victims" we have created and we will wonder why they do not change.

Chapter 8

Behavior

When children start dating or going out on their own at night it's a big step for a family. As parents, we're concerned about how our offspring will handle their new independence and we await their return with some anxiety. Gradually, as they meet curfews and act responsibly, we relax and become confident about our children's judgment and reliability. But one mishap or lie can shatter that confidence and make it difficult to restore it for a very long time.

When we realized that our daughter had lied about where she was going and who she was with on the night of the auto accident, we lost our confidence in her. Every time she went out we wondered, "What's next?" When the telephone rang we lifted the receiver with trepidation, half expecting another call from the hospital or perhaps the police. Although we talked with each other about our anxiety and tried to shut it out with sleep, we could only sleep lightly. Even if all went well one night, we would worry through the next. And when one daughter or another repeatedly came home late or stumbled about as if she had been drinking or smoking grass, we lost our confidence in ourselves.

We were anxious to get to work and apprehensive about returning home during those years. Work was our refuge. We never knew what we would find upon our return. Would the kids be home? Had they helped prepare dinner? Would some of their rowdy, rude friends be there? Would we have another confrontation? Often we would retreat to the upstairs of our home and leave the downstairs to them, just to avoid hassles.

The uneasiness was ever present although the incidents that caused it were intermittent. Perhaps Phyllis's new boots were missing or David's watch was misplaced. We'd ask who had been in the house. Our kids refused to believe that their friends were responsible for the missing objects. We worried and suspected but we didn't call the police. We didn't want to confront our own children as thieves and we didn't want to "get them in trouble." Not until our home was burglarized did we finally involve the police. Although we were certain that the culprits were our daughters' friends or enemies, they claimed they didn't know who it could be.

We never knew what would happen next, and the stress at home was oppressive. Phyllis constantly yelled, pleaded, and demanded, while David withdrew. To an outsider our behavior would have seemed very strange.

"Kids' behavior affects parents. Parents' behavior affects kids." The sixth of the Ten Beliefs may sound somewhat redundant but in reality parents' effect on their children receives far more credence and attention than their children's effect on them. For instance, when parents appear in the offices of juvenile probation, child welfare, or schools they often seem neurotic, if not downright crazy. "Aha," thinks the person behind the desk, "I can see why their kid acts like he does. These people have really screwed up their son."

We do not exaggerate when we say that many people, hidden safely behind their desks, forget they are seeing the parents after they've gone through hell and high water. Their perceptions are probably accurate: the parents' behavior is often very "nutsy." But in all likelihood parents were *not* that way before their child got into trouble.

People do not live in a vacuum. Their behavior is a product of interaction with their environment and when their environment, which includes their offspring, changes drastically, so do they. How irrational to expect parents to be calm and collected when they fear for their child's welfare, when they are frightened by violent and abusive acts, and when they see their son or daughter slipping deeper and deeper into trouble.

Ironically the culture accepts one side of the cause and effect relationship. "These people have really screwed up their son" is readily understood as an explanation for destructive behavior in the child. But try reversing the thought.

"Aha," thinks the person behind the desk, "I can see why his folks act like they do. This kid has really screwed up his parents."

Sounds strange, doesn't it? We're all used to thinking that parents' behavior affects their kids, not the reverse.

We are not arguing that a child's outrageous behavior "excuses" neurotic behavior in parents. Parents still can make choices about how they will respond to the situation, especially with the support of other parents with the same problem. We look back now at the time when our daughters were acting out and we recognize how foolish our behavior was. Others could have helped us see ourselves and ultimately they did.

David was the good guy in our family and Phyllis was the bad guy. Like on the day one of our girls brought home this sleazy fellow who made a Hell's Angel look good. Phyllis pulled her aside almost immediately and in her usual blunt style said what she thought of the guy. She told her that he was filthy, disgusting, rude, and secretive and that she didn't want him in our house.

When they left David told Phyllis that he thought she shouldn't be so harsh and abrupt and that she should be more respectful of her daughter's feelings. As usual at these times Phyllis got angry and told David that he didn't say a word when, in fact, he didn't like the guy either.

And we fought. Like every married couple our worst behavior would manifest itself when we were upset. Typically David would take the role of Mr. Calm-Cool-Collected and Phyllis would be Mrs. Sharp-Tongue-Anger. Phyllis expressed all the feelings and David all the reasonableness and we both accused each other of causing the problem while our daughter and her sleazy friend went on their merry way.

We went to see counselors at times like this and they would say to Phyllis in their best psychologese, "Look, Phyllis, your anger and quick response prevent David from speaking up, and David, your silence causes Phyllis to get angry and come on so heavy. Phyllis, why don't you try being quiet this week, and David, why don't you try speaking up." Phyllis would quickly agree while David strained to get out a nod of agreement.

The counselor didn't seem to realize that when one of our daughters appeared to be "going under" for the third time David was lucky if he could open his mouth to eat, let alone react verbally. He never realized how much support he needed to make such a simple change nor how much his anxiety and fear could clog his brain so that getting through the day was an effort. The counselor's advice was very appropriate in terms of David's behavior but it didn't help us with our feelings about our daughter.

What we have learned is that *first*, parents need help in reducing their anxiety about their children. Looking back, what we needed at this time was a third party who would intervene and tell us that we didn't have to accept our daughters' friends on their terms, and who would help us tell our daughters that they had to respect our values by not bringing raunchy people into our home.

Just giving advice isn't enough. Parents need *active* support in dealing with the problem before they can get around to changing husband-wife dynamics. The tactic works much more effectively than that of merely asking parents to change something about themselves and then hoping the kids will change.

In fact, once parents begin dealing with their kids' unacceptable behavior, the parents' extreme behavior diminishes. In our own life David is naturally quieter and Phyllis more verbal. We have adjusted to these patterns and we accept them. When David is anxious and starts to withdraw Phyllis can usually say, "What's going on with you? How can I help you?" and vice versa when Phyllis is anxious. But when the focus of anxiety is one of our kids we are both caught and then we feed off each other. At times like that we are at our worst and appear to be destructive and hurtful people.

No one can upset parents like their children. We

know that to be true from our personal experience as a family in crisis. But the counselors, school officials, probation officers, and caseworkers are in their professional roles when they meet troubled parents. Sitting calmly at their desks, they're in a position of power and they can make very important decisions without fully appreciating how it feels to be in the parents' situation: scared, distraught, arguing on the way there, fighting on the way home, finding themselves in a courtroom or hospital or jail or God knows where, a place that they have never been and that they hope and pray they will never be again.

Until our culture and the people who deal with troubled families recognize the reciprocity of parents' and kids' behavior, we are trapped in the same wheelspin, going nowhere fast. The events and actions of our children's lives, both good and bad, affect us. We are hooked into our children and we cry and laugh, mourn and rejoice with them. They can tug at our heartstrings, delight us, or make us anxious and distraught in an instant. Their power to influence us, particularly as adolescents in crisis, is no less than our power to influence them.

Chapter 9

Taking a Stand

In today's psychological culture the most typical approach to solving a personal or family problem is counseling. The drawback to counseling for a family that is suffering with a teenager's unacceptable behavior is that often the family does *not* have a psychological problem. The problem is cultural and needs a cultural solution.

All too often attempts at psychological solutions actually help feed and maintain the problem. Most psychological solutions rely on open, honest, and cooperative communication. Dependence on such modes of interaction enables insincere, manipulative people to continue their destructive behavior while they appear to be making changes. This is particularly true when the young person is involved in drug or alcohol abuse, a critical factor to consider when dealing with today's difficult adolescent. Traditional psychological approaches to drug and alcohol abuse have been markedly unsuccessful with chemical abusers of all ages. Counseling or even medication may be helpful for some people, perhaps essential, but only after the abuse has stopped. First the family, with the support of others, must stop the destructive behavior by taking a stand and precipitating a crisis for that young person.

"Taking a stand precipitates a crisis." The action orientation of TOUGHLOVE is based squarely on this seventh of the Ten Beliefs. Taking a stand and sticking to it is what makes TOUGHLOVE tough for parents to do. It's scary and new. It's what makes TOUGHLOVE controversial, but it's what makes TOUGHLOVE work.

Most families who come to a TOUGHLOVE group have tried a variety of other ways to solve their problem without success. If psychological approaches resolved the dilemma TOUGHLOVE would not even exist, for we tried several kinds of therapy in our own search for solutions before we realized that we had to do something different.

TOUGHLOVE involves others in the community who support parents through the difficult steps involved in confronting their son or daughter. In his book, *An Approach to Community Mental Health,* Gerald Caplan refers to "the importance of periods of crisis in determining individual and group development. Such a crisis is provoked when a person faces an obstacle to important life goals that is, for a time, insurmountable through the utilization of customary methods of problem-solving. A period of disorganization ensues, a period of upset, during which many abortive attempts at solution are made. Eventually some kind of adaptation is achieved, which may or may not be in the best interest of that person and his fellows." (New York: Behavioral Publications, 1974, p. 18.) The support of others and the structured recommendations of the TOUGHLOVE program help the parents find a new solution.

Let's return to the example of Betty and her daughter, June, discussed in Chapter 7. Betty has been thinking about the suggestion that Rachel and Bob made to allow her daughter June to take the responsibility for the fact that she cannot make her car payments despite June's promise to her mother that she would never miss any.

At her first TOUGHLOVE meeting, Betty was asked to do a crisis assessment. In the meeting that night she marked her responses on the checklist, which asked her questions like:

How often has your teenager come home:
( ) missing dinner
( ) high
( ) late

How often has your teenager run away:
( ) overnight
( ) two days
( ) a week

How often has your teenager been violent:
( ) verbally
( ) physically to the house or furniture
( ) physically to you or your spouse

How often have you or your spouse lost time from work because of your teenager?

How often have you not had a peaceful night's sleep?

How many times has your teenager been late for school?

How many fines has your teenager received?

How many drinking incidents has your teenager been charged with?

By recording her responses and determining whether the number of incidents was increasing or decreasing, Betty began to see the dimensions of her problem. She realized that she had been denying the extent of June's destructive behavior to herself because she found it so unbearable.

The crisis assessment concentrates on specific acts of behavior but avoids questions like "Why did you or anyone else do that?" and "What has or hasn't been done?" The *reasons* for people behaving in certain ways simply are not very useful right now. When the crisis is over everyone can explore the "whys" if they want. At the moment they only lead to confusion, blame, and helplessness.

The people entering TOUGHLOVE feel in crisis about what is happening in their family. The customary method of problem-solving, reasoning, scolding, punishing, and counseling have not worked. Each "adaptation," to use Caplan's word, has only momentarily eased the problem. The destructive behavior usually resumes and is more severe. The parents, as if numbed, tacitly accept each increased level without recognizing the growing crisis.

In our situation we gradually accepted sleazy friends, school failure, leaving school, car accidents, increasing disrespect, and lack of cooperation about simple household chores. From hindsight we are aware of these problems gradually increasing, but at the time we excused them as stages, self-esteem problems, or simply adolescent experimentation.

David is particularly adept at this kind of denial. His "good guy" visions of rainbows blotted out Phyllis's more realistic view of the storm. In fact one of the helpful things we eventually learned was for David to pay more attention to Phyllis's perception and act on that information, not his rose-colored view.

If we had assessed what was happening in our own family over a few months of any given year, we might have confronted ourselves earlier. We could have said, "Yes, we've had problems in all of these areas: school failures, fines, drunkenness, disorderly conduct, car accidents, staying out late without permission, bad faith lying, nastiness, laziness, missing household property, filthy rooms." But in our continued denial we tended to focus on the periods of quiet and the little, tiny signs of our kids' better nature. We kidded ourselves. Perhaps an assessment of the kind that TOUGHLOVE groups now do, pinpointing the things we hated to see, might have ended our plight much earlier. But without that assessment we searched for a solution to the disruptive behavior and found nothing that helped. So we adapted to an unsatisfactory way of life. We spent more time away from home and at our jobs and let our daughters come and go as they pleased.

TOUGHLOVE group members can be very helpful in supporting the crisis assessment and getting past denial by asking the new member to be as specific as possible about the behaviors they don't like and about the frequency with which they occur.

"She's been home late a few times," says the parent.

"How many times in the last month?" or "Exactly how late is she?" are the kinds of clarifying questions group members can ask. The object of this clarification process is not to expose dirty linen in public but to help parents see in black and white terms exactly what their problem is. Sharing this information with a group of caring and concerned people helps parents become realistic about what is happening in their family and exactly what behaviors are troubling them about their son or daughter. The outcome of this process leads to the point where parents "take a stand."

The act of taking a stand removes the ability of

destructive young people to generate crises for others and puts that power in the hands of parents. When used creatively and in concert with a TOUGHLOVE group the ability to create a crisis for these youths becomes a powerful and productive tool. The individual parents can do this crisis-generating procedure by themselves but their chances for success are far greater when they have the support of cooperative members of their community such as those involved in the TOUGHLOVE group.

When one of our daughters was arrested for holding up a dope dealer we took a stand. Our stand was that we would not accept criminal behavior. Two of our friends agreed to act as our support people. They went to jail where our daughter was being held for trial and determined that she was safe. They felt that getting bail money at this time would not be helpful since she still talked about what was happening as if it were an adventure. Meanwhile the prison psychologist was calling us and telling us that our daughter wasn't like the other women and that we should get her out. We listened to our friends instead and they helped us resist our guilt and stick to our stand.

Our hope is that parents won't wait as long as we did and that out of the assessment will come the issues upon which to base the stand. In Betty's case she had already made an "adaptation" by allowing her daughter to quit school, so she doesn't really have to deal with school issues anymore. But other issues are plentiful, centering around her daughter's not coming home on time, not being financially responsible, and being verbally abusive. Betty also suspects that her daughter is increasingly using drugs. Since speaking with Rachel and Bob she decided to bring the money issue up with the group and ask other people's advice.

"How many times has your daughter missed car payments?"

"This will be the third time. I just don't have the money to keep laying out for her. She still owes me for the two previous payments she missed."

"It sounds like you really want to take a stand on this issue," says Rachel.

Betty nods. "Yes, I think I do. I've been thinking about it since we talked. You have suggested that I make an 'I will not' statement about the issue. And I think I can now."

The group supports her in the choice she makes. Her stand is "I will not accept my daughter's financial responsibilities anymore." Betty's stand, like most people's, coincides with a pressing problem which allows for some immediate action.

Some stands that people have taken in TOUGHLOVE groups are:

"I will not have a drunken or stoned child living in my house."

"I will not allow my daughter to keep returning after running away from home."

"We will not allow our son to curse in our home anymore."

"I will not accept physical abuse from my kid."

A stand is a long-term goal. However, most parents, when they take a stand, want to get there right away. They have spelled out how awful things are at home in front of others and all the anger, hurt, and embarrassed feelings rush in. But reaching a goal takes planning, structure, and *then* action.

The function of taking a stand is to define the area in which parents are now willing to precipitate a crisis for their young person. The TOUGHLOVE group becomes very important since the crisis is going to be of the parents' making and they will need the concern, caring, humor, creativity, and support of others. Although the crisis is for the purpose of bringing about a solution, it is very difficult to endure alone.

Chapter 10

Controlled Crisis

The Chinese have a symbol for the English word "crisis" that is made with two characters: one stands for danger and the other for opportunity. When we have been faced with the danger of those crises produced by our children, it is useful for us to think about the Chinese symbol and contemplate the opportunity side of crisis.

Most parents who come to TOUGHLOVE only see the potential for danger. They say, "At least when my kid comes home drunk I know he's not lying on the highway somewhere," or "If I hassle my daughter about running away maybe she won't come back and she'll end up a prostitute in New York City," or "It's better that my kid expresses his anger verbally to me than by hurting someone else physically." Each one of these fear statements includes elements of truth; the fears are all based on real possibility. But as long as parents focus on the danger they will remain unaware of the opportunity for positive change inherent in each crisis.

Fear is precisely what empowers the youth to manipulate his or her family and keeps the family feeling that they are being controlled by a destructive youth. To turn the tide some tough steps must be taken, steps which are in many ways tougher on the parents than they are on the child.

Studies have shown the effects of such a crisis may last anywhere from four to six weeks and that as a result of crisis resolution people can make dramatic and sweeping changes in their lives, changes that years of psychotherapy have not accomplished. TOUGHLOVE can help parents end the kind of crisis that keeps them helpless and focus the consequences of harmful behavior on the person who is responsible.

In effect, we are recommending that parents give their children the crisis, instead of hanging on to it. We finally took action when our daughter committed armed robbery. The fact that she stole from a dope dealer didn't make any difference. We decided that we had rescued her far too often. This time we backed off and refused to supply bail, a lawyer, or emotional and moral support. That's how we gave her back the crisis.

Ordinarily parents like us rush to save our child from the horrors of prison and the stigma of arrest. By refusing to do so we allow a harmful and unlawful youth to fully experience the consequences of her actions. The youth now has to handle the situation and it becomes a meaningful learning experience.

Like most loving parents we couldn't just walk away from our child. We felt horrible. We asked friends to help us and by doing so created the first informal TOUGHLOVE group. Our friends supported us emotionally and checked on our daughter, visiting her and seeing that she was as safe as possible under the circumstances. They gave her information and advice, but they were careful not to "rescue" her. The resolution of the crisis was up to her.

That is exactly how the TOUGHLOVE groups work. After a parent has decided to take a stand the stage is set for a crisis to occur. In our case our stand was "We will not accept criminal behavior." Our daughter now had to avoid breaking the law or accept the consequences. In another situation, which we will more fully describe, parents took the stand that they would not allow their eighteen-year-old son constantly to come home drunk. Now their son would have to be more responsible with his use of alcohol.

Once parents have taken a stand, the TOUGHLOVE group asks the parents to set a "bottom line." The bottom line is a small step that will move the parents toward implementation of their stand. It is important that parents initiate and maintain their bottom line commitment for the week until the next meeting. The group tries to help them avoid failure by asking parents how they can support them. (On the other hand failure is not a mortal sin and parents should not be so intimidated by their fellow group members that they can't come back to the group. Parents should just keep coming and try again.)

In the case of the eighteen-year-old drunk, the family agreed that they would take action after five more binges. That was their bottom line: five more and then action. Perhaps it seems like a weak approach but that's what the parents could tolerate and other group members said they would be willing to support them. It's better to make a bottom line that people can actually handle than to force a bottom line that's too tough for them to keep. After all, the agreement only lasts a week and people can get progressively tougher as they gain strength from their own changed behavior and their growing trust in the TOUGHLOVE group's support.

Further defining the bottom line and the support they would receive from their group, the parents decided that after their son came home drunk a fifth time they would refuse to permit him to stay in their home until he had a drug and alcohol evaluation and agreed to follow the evaluator's recommendations. A group member who lived on the next block agreed that she would call every day to see how things were going and that she would be available to take their son to the evaluation while another family agreed to provide a place for him to stay if necessary.

Five days after the meeting the young man had accomplished his fifth drunk. The parents were both furious and terrified: furious that he hadn't stayed sober even one day, terrified about insisting that he have a drug and alcohol evaluation, a confrontation which might (at least in their fears) drive him away to become a derelict.

The support person was on her way over when she met the young man carrying a duffel bag. He reported that he was going to live at a friend's house and he didn't want or need her help. He wasn't heard from for four days.

What a frightening and trying time for the parents. They were overwhelmed with doubt, fear, and anger. As people do during such anxious periods, the parents also became very blaming. Blaming themselves for taking such drastic action, blaming the TOUGHLOVE group for encouraging them to do so, blaming anyone and everyone.

The group members understood the anxiety, many having had similar experiences. They called, came over, checked with the boy's friends, the police, and hospitals, but mostly encouraged the parents to persist. They had taken a stand and precipitated a crisis. They were now in a position to control that crisis and create positive change, but the next move was up to their son.

On the fourth day they received a collect call from their son in Los Angeles. (They lived in New Jersey.) Their son informed them that he had hitchhiked to the West Coast and tried to find a job. There was no work available, said he, and he wanted money to come home. His mom got his telephone number and said that she would call him back shortly.

Mom called her support people for advice. At first she was encouraged to tell him to hitchhike home, since that's the way he got there, but that was more than she and her husband could bear. So they settled on sending him a one-way, nonrefundable (a wise precaution) bus ticket.

When the bus arrived in Trenton at two in the morning, four TOUGHLOVE parents plus his own were at the station to meet him. They all went to another family's home and worked out a temporary arrangement under which he could return home. The plan included: absolutely no drinking, finishing his last semester of high school, working for one of the TOUGHLOVE members to earn enough to pay his parents for the bus ticket, and weekly reporting to another TOUGHLOVE dad on how he was doing with his commitments.

We caution readers to realize that the family did not ride off into the sunset, happily ever after. There were still problems, as there are in all families. But the drunkenness and its extremely harmful effect on the normal ebb and flow of family life ended.

Not all situations go to such an extreme. In most situations the resolution is much less dramatic, but in a few cases it still has not occurred after several years. Even in these latter few situations where young people have chosen not to accept the way their family wants them to live, the disruption and destruction has left the family's everyday life. Other children in the family are no longer angry and confused and the fighting and recriminations between parents have drastically diminished.

The parents still ache at their loss, but they feel resolved that the choice was their son's or daughter's decision, not theirs. They will always be available should their child want to return as a real member of the family.

"From controlled crisis comes positive change" is the eighth of our Ten Beliefs. Until now most of the families who have used the TOUGHLOVE technique for creating a crisis and controlling the crisis with the help of a TOUGHLOVE group have accomplished positive results. Being aware of both the danger and the opportunity, many families have generated a crisis for their unruly child and found that the ultimate benefits are well worth the risk.

Chapter 11

Community Support

The worst time of our lives began just before Christmas. Our daughter's behavior had been deteriorating for a long time but we continued to rescue her—until that fateful telephone call. We realized when she wasn't home yet that something was wrong. But we were not prepared.

"Hello, Mom, I'm at the police station. I need money for bail."

"You've been arrested? What happened?"

"It's this dealer. It's all a mistake. I need bail money."

We looked at each other and we didn't even have to discuss the matter. We now knew that we'd been handling everything all wrong. We had to change directions.

"I'm sorry but I can't help you. I work with people like you but I don't live with them."

"But Ma, you don't want me to go to jail. It's a mistake."

"I can't help you."

Horror. Disbelief. Fear. Bewilderment. Anger. Sorrow. We cried and cried. We talked. We hid in sleep. We called our friend Mary who said she'd go see her.

Phyllis remembers thinking that she wouldn't see a

child of hers in jail. She felt like sitting shiva (a Jewish death ritual) for her daughter. How could she face people, her clients? Who was she to help others? How could we have Christmas?

We told our other daughters. One seemed tough, accepting, muttering things around the house about "it's her life," angering us with her calmness. She began to bake Christmas cookies, then gave way to her frightened feelings and admitted that her sister went too far. But she still insisted that we put up bail. The other cried. But she was busy with a new boyfriend. What did she feel when she told him? He was surprised, to say the least.

When we went to work the next day Phyllis burst into tears and Teresa, our coworker, held her in her arms. Teresa and Mary began to work out plans for bail and help, keeping us out of it. Looking back we realize how critical their support was to us.

Our daughter called and we rejected her. She had to deal with our support people, Mary and Teresa. Her sister threatened to get bail for her and we actually pulled her to the floor and sat on her.

"I'll kill you," Phyllis screamed. "You will not get her bail."

Our daughter called again and again, but we refused to see her. We made no decisions without Mary and Teresa.

Christmas Eve was depressing. Mary and Teresa and a few others came to our house, but our grief and worry consumed us. How do you celebrate Christmas picturing your daughter in jail? In our minds she seemed so little and vulnerable. We wanted to help her and knew we shouldn't. What a paradox when parents both fear their child and fear for her. Our friends' support was thorough. They developed a plan and we agreed. Mary would put up bail and attend the trial. They would arrange for her to enter a rehabilitation center. We stayed out of the way and cried a lot.

Then David broke his ankle.

It's strange what mixed feelings one has sometimes. Phyllis recalls feeling sorry for him but her primary feeling was anger at being abandoned. She had no one to be dependent on. She remembers thinking during that short ambulance ride, "Our daughter's in jail, David's going to the hospital, and Phyllis is left holding the bag. What else could possibly go wrong?"

Plenty. A few days later was David's birthday and he was awaiting an operation on his ankle. A "For Sale" sign on the lawn led to the discovery that our landlord had declared bankruptcy and had given up the property without telling anyone we lived there. While Phyllis and our daughters prepared a birthday dinner of filet mignon and all the fixings to take to the hospital, the heat went off in the house. It was the oil man who informed us, as we left for the hospital, that the garage was flooded because the plumbing had burst. When we got to the hospital David was in such pain that he couldn't eat a thing.

Some days go better than others. Support makes the tough times easier. But there are people who don't know when support is appropriate. Like the counselor who came to see us about a week after David returned home.

The young woman, who was doing her graduate internship at the rehab where our daughter now lived, took it upon herself to visit us. She let us know that we were ridiculous not to see our daughter, that she was really a good kid, that our daughter knew our friends

Mary and Teresa were just stand-ins, and that we ought to realize our responsibility to her.

David told her that she didn't know what she was talking about and Phyllis told her to get out. As she buttoned her coat Phyllis asked her if she couldn't see that we were in pain and trying to do what we thought was right; that our daughter had to prove she wanted us first.

She replied, "Well, I'm only a student!"

"I know," said Phyllis as she slammed the door.

Her visit and report to her teachers and supervisors must have clarified why our poor daughter was so screwed up.

But our friends were supportive through thick and thin. Without their help we could not have endured our daughter's ordeal the way we did. Mary delivered her clothes when she went to the rehab and spoke to her regularly on the telephone. A friend took her to lunch. Teresa reassured us.

So we came to our ninth TOUGHLOVE belief, "Families need to give and get support in their own community in order to change." We were only able to sustain our change in behavior toward our daughter because we had support and we have seen countless examples of that since.

When a child is picked up by the police and parents have to go down to get him and the TOUGHLOVE group sends people with them or for them, that's support.

When the policemen empathize with the parents because they know the group will follow through and the charges are pressed because the magistrate knows he can fine the child and others will see that he or she pays, that's support.

When a county caseworker can call a TOUGHLOVE group member late on a Friday afternoon and get temporary housing for a youth in an extenuating circumstance, that's support.

When a TOUGHLOVE couple offers use of their summer home to another couple and baby-sitting for their younger children because they need a break, that's support.

When a friend makes the arrangements for another person whose child must be committed to a psychiatric hospital for the fourth time, that's support.

When someone goes to the public school to establish a plan for someone else who must be at work, that's support.

When people negotiate with parents and child to arrange for his or her return home, that's support.

When parents go to the hospital or jail for other parents, that's support.

When someone sits and listens to another person's fears and sorrow and helps him or her develop a plan of action, that's support.

Support is not always easy or convenient. It can be demanding and time consuming. We're not talking about a pat on the back or quick words of wisdom. We're talking about support that is selective and knowledgeable and frequently confrontative.

Supportive confrontation is the kind of support that people find most difficult, yet it's extremely important, perhaps the most important kind of support because it gets the individual and the TOUGHLOVE group moving.

Supportive confrontation is saying what's really on one's mind, not saving it for later and talking behind the person's back. That kind of behavior can destroy a TOUGHLOVE group by trampling trust among members.

"I think you're marvelously helpful to others in the group, Louise, but you're very secretive about your own problems. What's happening in your life?" Louise may not like what she's hearing but that kind of support will help her, not harm her. The best that we can do for someone is to act as an honest mirror, even if we reflect warts and mussed up hair.

"You two are always arguing. If you're going to help your kid you have to get together. After your kid's O.K. you can fight all you want."

Or, "I know you love your kid but defending your own drinking problem gets in the way of helping your son with his drug abuse."

Or, "After we made the arrangement for your son to pick up his clothes at my house you screwed up the deal. I can't be your support person anymore because you've undermined my credibility with your kid."

Tough things to say, but that's TOUGHLOVE. It's real, not phony, and it gets to the heart of the matter. People who only want to be "nice" to each other are not really being nice. Their silence about real issues withholds the kind of help that does the most good.

Supportive confrontation is what TOUGHLOVE offers to parents and their children so that they can develop new behaviors and discard old ones. At the risk of not being "liked" by others, we help them see what's really happening and enable them to grow. It's a loving, challenging, caring way to provoke change.

But supportive confrontation is selective, as are other kinds of support. TOUGHLOVE does not work indiscriminately. We choose to support some actions and attitudes and challenge others. We do not support guilt, blame, indulgence, fear, mollycoddling, or psychological excuses. We do support limit setting, taking a stand, and small bottom line steps to large goals.

We support finding ways to cooperate with social service agencies and the legal system so that children experience consequences for unacceptable behavior. We support parents in recognizing drug and alcohol abusing behaviors. We support standing up to our children's manipulations. We support children in stopping their harmful deeds.

We do not support the use of counselors who "psychologize" the problem but we encourage the patronage of counselors who will cooperate with our TOUGHLOVE strategies. We are willing to pick and choose carefully.

The kind of support practiced by TOUGHLOVE can apply to the community at large. A supportive community can meet the needs of its individual members by developing structures and systems that are nonblaming and cooperative.

But our culture has lost its sense of "neighborhood." Perhaps it still exists in some places, but for the most part we are an independent, mobile, and highly competitive people who have a great deal of difficulty asking our next-door neighbors for help. We are stuck in our pride, afraid of embarrassment, isolated and unsupported in our own communities.

Ironically the youthful peer group that engages in the kinds of behaviors which TOUGHLOVE counters is more mutually supportive than the adults in our communities. For example, in New Hope, Pennsylvania, where the first TOUGHLOVE parent/community support group was founded in 1978, we found that teenagers knew far more about each other than their parents.

Assisted by compulsory schooling these young people were brought together every day and they had numerous opportunities to collude in bypassing parental authority.

We found that the adolescents would lie for each other and coordinate stories so that parents were totally duped. A boy who was avoiding his parents' wrath would stay at another boy's house under the guise of avoiding his parents' horrible behavior. "Oh, Mom, his parents are constantly arguing." Wanting to be a "good parent" Mom would buy the story without checking on its truthfulness with the boy's parents. To the teenagers it must have been hilarious how gullible parents could be.

The adults' isolation from one another was their children's greatest ally. Failing to cooperate and support one another, adults remained powerless. When they finally got together and began to see what was going on, the teens were frightened and intimidated. Stolen property began to reappear on people's doorsteps. Lies and excuses no longer held up.

By supporting one another parents regained their authority and dramatic changes began to occur in their sons and daughters. Faced with the consequences of their actions, no longer able to hide behind their parents' confusion, many of the young people recognized the need to "get their acts together." And they did.

Without support in his or her own community, each parent would have struggled on, with nothing changing. Our experience in New Hope confirmed our belief that support is critical for success and we have spread the word to others as TOUGHLOVE groups spring up around the country, uniting parents with common needs. Our dream is that TOUGHLOVE can model a new approach to other kinds of local needs as well, encouraging the development of mutually supportive communities.

Chapter 12

Cooperation

The best time of our lives began just before Christmas. Our daughters were six, eight, and ten and we were living in rural Vermont. We had just moved into our newly renovated home, a big country house on a hill with a panoramic view that stretched beyond the Green Mountains to Canada in the distance. We were caught up in the excitement of the holiday season, five feet of snow, and the anticipation of old friends coming to visit from New York City.

A huge Scotch pine dominated our living room. David and the girls had to cut several feet from the bottom of the tree after dragging it from the nearby woods, for in their enthusiasm they had misjudged its height. We baked a thousand Christmas cookies, bundled ourselves up, and tromped down snowy roads delivering the goodies to neighbors. Native Vermonters who seemed a hundred years old invited us to sit and rock for a spell by their woodstoves before we continued our rounds.

We recall that winter's images like fantasies: the kids jumping rope in the basement where their rabbits were nestled safe from the cold, a little girl nursing a sick bunny, sobs and tears when it died, hot chocolate and cookies, bedtime stories, clear moonlit nights in an idyllic setting.

How starkly that winter in Vermont contrasts in our memories with the winter in Pennsylvania when our daughter went to jail. Where did we go wrong? How did we fail? We belabored those questions for a long time and now believe we have some possible answers. Answers that lie in our Ten Beliefs, not the least of which is the tenth, "The essence of family life is cooperation, not togetherness." Cooperation values people working together to make family life easier and more pleasant for everyone. Togetherness, as we use it, values people for their availability as love objects, the kind of love we give to newborn babies, very young children, and puppies. Togetherness is child-centered, whereas cooperation is people-centered.

Togetherness, when sought from acting-out teenagers, proves to be destructive because it treats them like infants, valuing them for the mere act of being. We became aware of the danger of this when we worked with teenagers in drug rehabilitation centers. We were often struck by their grandiose schemes. Living in a daydream world, buoyed by their artificial stimuli, many teens told us their career plans to be rock stars. When we asked them how that would come about they revealed their naïve notions about "being discovered" without any real effort on their part. Most of them got no further than buying guitars and amplifiers and one young fellow persisted in his delusions even after he foolishly traded his guitar for a bag of grass. Somehow, even without their drugs, they had an inflated sense of their own worth. A generation of children who feel valued without fulfilling any real demands.

Cooperation, on the other hand, is based on the acceptance of leadership and a family hierarchy that functions for the good of all. When parents cope with young people who treat the family with an "I'm just doing my thing, man" attitude, they need to take a strong leadership position. A position that says, "We are a cooperative family that lives and works together and doing your own thing at our expense will not be tolerated." Parents must take a stand against abuse by stressing what young people must do to have access to family resources. Destructive young people must learn that there is no free lunch.

We do *not* speak to the issues of child rearing in general or to issues that apply in all times. We speak about our culture in the here and now. For it changes quickly and our solution to negative young people may soon be obsolete. Our guess is that the tug of peers in our daughters' teenage years proved more powerful than the values of their family. In light of the events of the sixties and seventies which undermined authority and tradition, our culture swung from the extreme of the past, when children were to be seen but not heard, to another extreme in which children are always to be heard, even if everyone else had to stop their conversation. Surely children are important, but when we look back on our own experience we feel that we left our children with the impression that they were the center of the universe.

It's not that we made no demands on our daughters when they were young. There was a time when cooperation existed, when our kids picked up their toys, set the table, washed dishes, and saved pennies to buy presents. They knew they were cared about and they cared for others. We insisted that they develop responsibility and do things for themselves and others. When they reached their teens we thought they were prepared for the outside world and we increasingly focused on our careers and our own development, not recognizing the demands new values and new environments would place on them.

Had we stayed in Vermont, somewhat insulated from our rapidly changing culture, perhaps things would have been different, perhaps not. But we moved on. What might have made Vermont different was its more stable and supportive community environment. Although we tried to maintain a loving, caring family wherever we were, believing that the kind of "togetherness" we had in Vermont and elsewhere would guarantee loving, caring teenagers, we did not fully appreciate the other factors in our daughters' and our own lives. Although our daughters had learned a great deal about loving and caring, when they became teenagers they applied what they had learned, without discrimination, to their friends and forgot about their parents.

When we were trying to live cooperatively with one of our daughters and she was treating us like the enemy, we felt used, abused, and angry. She would agree to go to a family function, do a chore, or run an errand, but somehow it never worked out. She always had some reason or excuse for not fulfilling her agreements. She would use a family car to go to work but somehow could never afford to pay for its maintenance. She agreed to pay rent, but somehow never had the full amount or would ask us to wait until next week.

Finally we stopped being suckers and stopped helping her to maintain a lifestyle that was supported by us but gave nothing back. We sat down with her and said that either she pay her rent on the upcoming Friday when she got paid or give us her car keys, pack her bags, and leave. Friday she called and said she was going roller-skating and we repeated our demands. Saturday afternoon when she came home she looked ready to fight, but we just restated our demands: "Leave the car keys and be gone when we get home." We left the house in agony but knew our nineteen-year-old daughter had given us no choice.

She moved in with her sister for a while and then with another friend. A year and a half later she asked to move back home until she could decide what she wanted to do next. We had seen changes over the past year: a recognition that if she wanted our friendship she would have to call us, celebrate family events with us, and stick to agreements she made with us. She had started to talk to us like real people. We agreed to her return home to see if cooperation would work this time.

We've had our angry times, like when she couldn't get a ride to work and tried to put the responsibility and blame on us. But she called up an hour later and said she was wrong. She is honest about where she goes and what she is doing. She goes shopping and helps with the cooking and dishes without being asked. She is friendly to our friends and seeks out our company. No, we don't agree with everything she does and says, but we do live together cooperatively. The important point is that by demanding cooperation we have been able to move toward a caring, close, and friendly relationship with our daughter. But by acting as if our daughter was caring, close, and friendly when she really wasn't, we ended up abused and angry.

We parents get confused about what family life is all

about. We thought that we would get cooperation by having a loving, caring family with lots of togetherness, and perhaps that was true when the culture around us shared those values. In the world that existed when our daughters reached the relative independence of their teens, all of our efforts at preparing them seemed in vain. With the challenges of changing times it seems that we needed to take a stronger stand than we did, especially when they began to get in trouble, rather than rely on reasonableness and understanding.

The way you get cooperation from unruly young people is to withdraw the family resources which allow them to exploit their parents. By our insisting that they recognize their obligations to the family and its needs as a whole unit, young people will practice mutuality. We must value ourselves as much as we value our children.

Cooperation is based on respect for everyone in the family and is accomplished by asking every family member to do his or her share of the tasks needed for maintenance and control of the family. But the individual family cannot achieve that goal without support from the community at large. When our daughters became teenagers, cooperation and good feelings waned despite all our past and continuing efforts. We were not prepared, in all of our life experience, for the kind of defiance and disdain for others that prevailed in the newly developing youth culture.

When parents of acting-out young people are told, as we were, to be more understanding and to listen and try to be reasonable without demanding anything of their children, it only intensifies the problem. If they follow this advice, they further enhance their children's unrealistic sense of their own importance and encourage their destructiveness and inconsideration for everyone else.

The point is that destructive young people are "bad faith" negotiators. Their interests and values are with their friends, dope, and things outside the family. Their home is perceived as a place where they occasionally withdraw from real life. Not until this attitude is confronted and they recognize their dependence on their family will change occur. We, as much as any parent, helped distort our children's perceptions of themselves by failing to ask more of them.

Once in crisis, parents cling to their memories of those wonderful childhood years of togetherness and good feeling. Thinking that they can achieve that togetherness again, they appease their teenagers and have as much success as Chamberlain had with Hitler.

We know two different families whose children chose to leave their homes because their parents refused to tolerate repeatedly unacceptable behavior. Even having taken such strong stands, the parents invited these young people to family gatherings on the chance that the "togetherness" of the gathering would persuade that son or daughter to change his or her ways and choose to "belong" to the family again. Their hopes were cruelly dashed when both wayward children, in separate instances, stole from relatives at the family events.

Social service agencies are mandated to keep the family intact because theory stresses the abuses and costs of institutionalization of children. Resisting even temporary separation of acting-out youths from their families as a strategic maneuver, the agencies cling to the notion that out of togetherness will come cooperation.

It just isn't so, for these kinds of young people come to "togetherness" in bad faith and use understanding and kindness as an opportunity to manipulate.

In the past, togetherness was associated with certain kinds of family rituals. For example, "the family that prays together stays together." The family dinner is another ritual that provided a time for intimacy and communication. These rituals not only gave structure to family life but gave us a feeling of closeness. Rituals were outward signs of family unity. But as our culture shifts, rituals can become empty and meaningless.

Phyllis remembers her mother lighting *shabbas* candles each Friday night, the Jewish holidays, dressing up to attend services at the synagogue, and the undercurrent of family tension and the arguments, as well as the warmth. But the meaning of these compulsory rituals was somehow lost in her Americanization. Our family's major holidays are now limited to Thanksgiving, Christmas, and Passover and they're still not the "perfect" family gatherings.

In abandoning our rituals we abandoned our symbols and structures for intimacy. We complain that there is no time for each other, that our families don't do things together and everyone goes his or her own way. Especially when children become teenagers, the common cry is that we're not intimate enough. The expectations of what family members should be to one another have increased and intimacy today doesn't have the same meaning it did fifty years ago. Our rituals gave family life boundaries for intimacy but now there are no clear limits and we are very confused.

The pressure on people to be intimate, to have "hot," intense relationships, is very strong. Just read today's women's magazines or the "family" or "living" sections of the daily newspaper. They urge people to be open, honest, communicative, frank, sensitive, and assertive. These cultural demands, without the "coolness" of a ritualized structure, are overwhelming for many families and simply getting away from each other in a nonhurtful way can be a real dilemma.

Today our culture insists that parents and children share everything. If you are a parent you *should* be able to talk to your kid (knowledgeably) about sex, drugs, and feelings, and God forbid that you aren't comfortable discussing those subjects. People who promote such forced intimacy may have forgotten that there are young folks who are embarrassed to discuss things with their parents.

Some friends reported that when they approached their son to discuss sex, as they thought they should, he responded almost pleadingly, "Do I have to know all about that stuff now?" They backed off realizing that they were contriving to meet cultural expectations for their family and at least at this time, it was not appropriate.

TOUGHLOVE asks people to stop indulging themselves in cultural fantasies: fantasies that the family's problem is unique, fantasies that the family can solve its own problems (albeit with a private school or private therapy), fantasies that what is needed is more togetherness. For ultimately it is action taken in concert with other members of our community that will stop the spiral of destruction and begin movement toward a cooperative family.

Cooperation is not based on being or feeling loved, but on a mutual sense of responsibility. Doing household chores, for instance, is one way of maintaining the family for everyone. Cooperation requires that individual family members stop indulging themselves in the luxury of competition. Refusing to take out the garbage, either directly or indirectly by "forgetting," is a win-lose competitive situation based on personal rivalry. "Why do I have to take out the garbage? John doesn't do it." These statements get parents caught in explaining why and are really ways of circumventing cooperation.

More often uncooperative adolescents are less direct. They remain silent when asked and later say, "Oh, I forgot." Whether they are verbal or not, their resistance is calculated to frustrate parents until they take out the garbage themselves to avoid the hassle.

Competition like this springs from the willingness of parents to explain *why* children should help and *how* they as parents are trying to be fair to each kid. Their reasonableness and fairness keep them trapped in the competitive game. Cooperative teenagers don't need explanations and frequent reminders; they have a cooperative spirit. They recognize their dependency on their parents even though they may not always like it. With acting-out young people, parents find themselves trying to abide by the rules of fairness while their kids really are playing with different rules.

With such young people we need to stop the games and provide clear consequences for their behavior. No more explanations, just straightforward demands for cooperation. Unless such lines are drawn there is a big payoff for hassling Mom and Dad. The payoff occurs because we have valued children wanting to be with us rather than children working with us. Cooperation occurs when the rewards for cooperating are greater than the rewards for competing.

The same principles apply beyond the family. As long as the social service agencies, schools, police, courts, mental health professionals, therapists, and counselors are trying to achieve cooperation by being "reasonable" or by fostering togetherness, we are stuck with selfish, destructive kids. Parents cannot set limits for acting-out children if the community does not support them. When parents' authority and credibility is undermined by established institutions and professionals they are severely handicapped in their efforts. But with nonblaming attitudes, shared goals, and common strategies, communities can support parents in taking the tough stands needed to get cooperation instead of unacceptable behavior from their children.

Part III

THE TOUGHLOVE PROCESS

Chapter 13

Process of Change

"This must be a phase the kids are going through."

"It feels like we have street behavior in our home, but it can't be. My kids aren't like the people I treat."

"It must be me, I'm an unhappy person."

All these statements denied the reality of horror we were experiencing in our own lives. Over the years we can remember hating to sit down to a meal with our children. The kids sometimes wouldn't talk or they'd fool around, giggling, avoiding discussion, and avoiding us. Sometimes secretive, they would be angry and sullen. Sometimes they would be extremely playful. Sometimes one would sing at us telling us with the words of a song that we would never understand her and that she would not speak to us. Always manipulative. There were those terrible events like stops at the police station to pick up a drunk kid, with tears and fights afterward. All those nights fearing that one kid or another had been in an accident. Or the time one daughter gave another a black eye. And the relief when we'd come home and everyone was out, a reprieve from arguing about tasks not done.

At the beginning we thought it was "adolescent rebellion." We thought, "All kids experiment with drugs," or "It must be painful for them in a new school," or "They must be angry at us for moving again." When they didn't want to go visiting with us we felt it was because they were getting older but soon we felt avoided, dismissed, and helpless. But even then we thought we must be crazy. Phyllis found herself thinking that since David didn't seem too annoyed, then maybe she was the problem, always yelling, always dissatisfied.

Even the one daughter who was doing well kept getting lost in all the havoc. And when she'd behave selfishly it was like a last straw. She'd fight and argue with her sisters all the time.

Gradually we avoided each other: one daughter went off to college, another moved out to live with a friend, the third came and went as she pleased while we hid in work. Our attempts at counseling, private schools, or tutoring always aborted.

We managed to deny to ourselves and others the realities of our family life for years. Denial, considered a primitive psychological defense, can more accurately be thought of as lying: lying to others and ourselves about what is happening. Our lies protect our self-images and our values, keeping us trapped in deleterious behavior while covering up our helplessness.

David was so self-deceptive that he turned piranhas into goldfish. He did this by focusing on each problem as it arose. If a daughter was picked up for shoplifting, received a fine for disorderly conduct, had trouble in school, or ended up in the drunk tank, he would deal with the problem as an isolated incident.

He would sit down with his kid and try to find out

what was bothering her. Did she feel bad about not having dates, doing poorly in school, having trouble with friends? He would work out a "solution" with her or she would talk to a counselor or our whole family would go to a counselor or we would go to school and talk to her teachers.

Each situation would get resolved individually and he would never see the dimensions of the whole crisis, believing that she was just having a good time or the authorities were picking on her or these were just the problems of growing up. He breathed a sigh of relief after each incident, telling himself what a great understanding dad he was.

David's self-deception gave him an air of calmness and control while Phyllis's sharp and volatile responses made her seem like the complaining shrew. David was the good guy, Phyllis was the bad guy.

Phyllis felt there must be something wrong with her since she was sad or mad at the kids all the time and David wasn't. She lied to herself by accepting David's view of reality, rather than her own.

Friends of ours would make observations but we usually managed to ignore them. For instance our colleague Eliot, a bachelor, would make wisecracks like, "If they were my kids I'd give them away." But we dismissed what he said because, after all, what did he know if he wasn't a parent?

We tried to deny what was going on because we didn't know what to do about it. We had false hope in thinking that maybe if we left our daughters alone they would grow out of their behavior. Without an apparent solution we protected ourselves from our feelings of helplessness at almost any cost.

Had someone asked us to sit down to assess the crisis as a whole, as TOUGHLOVE groups do, to list the events that plagued us, and to examine how we handled them, our self-deception might have crumbled. Instead it took the police coming to our house with shotguns and an arrest warrant for our daughter to make our denial obvious. David, the good guy, couldn't clean this situation up and Phyllis, the bad guy, recognized the accuracy of her sad and mad feelings.

In retrospect it seems strange that we needed such powerful prodding to get out of our patterns, but recognizing and accepting the need for change is awfully difficult. What made change even harder was that we had to question what we had come to believe from people we admired: learned people who expressed ideas and values about how parents and children should be, writers whose books were challenging and exciting, experts who told us that the kids of the technological age would be so different that we would not understand them. We used all this information and our own idiosyncrasies to build our family and it was tough to accept that our best intentions, liberally doused with love and caring, didn't give us kids who reciprocated in kind.

TOUGHLOVE groups are designed to help parents move from denying the reality of their family life to facing what's happening. It's pretty hard to avoid looking at problem patterns when ten or twelve other parents are helping you and comparing notes and even predicting what will happen next week or next month. It's a powerful and eye-opening experience when you hear people describing your kid's kind of behavior in their own households and you begin to realize that it's not just you but a phenomenon that's sweeping the whole society.

"It's only a stage," or "She has so much potential." Those clichés get harder to say in the company of other parents who have also denied the same patterns and have made molehills out of mountains the size of the Himalayas.

Accepting the destruction you have been living with brings up strong feelings within you but no one can be more appropriately supportive than parents who have had the same experience. Instead of feeling threatened by a "holier than thou" attitude, either real or imagined, parents feel the camaraderie of others who have "been there" too. Perhaps the old adage that misery loves company applies but the atmosphere of TOUGHLOVE groups fosters action and change, not more misery.

The act of sharing with others our hurt and the disrespect and abuse that we have allowed because we love our children forces us to face and accept the failure of this way of loving: a way of loving that hides the truth and at the same time supports unacceptable behavior. Going public isn't easy. No matter how often we talk about our daughter getting arrested and going to jail it's still emotionally traumatic. But we also know that by sharing we confirm our resolve that we will never go through that kind of experience again.

When we came home from work on that fateful day we were angry that our daughter had left the house despite her promise to remain at home. At our lawyer's advice she was waiting until after the Christmas holidays to respond to an arrest warrant by turning herself in to the police.

Our hearts almost stopped when she called and told us that she was arrested for another offense. We felt furious, betrayed, and then empty. Saying, "No, we won't help you," we felt our powerlessness and recognized the void that existed. We had given up our false hope and had no energy left. We stood in the kitchen, holding each other and crying.

But we realized that we would not go on making the same mistakes. We called our friends, Mary and Teresa, told them what happened, and asked them to take over for us. They agreed. In doing so we finally moved past denial into dependence and began to rely on others, accepting our own helplessness. For parents who come to TOUGHLOVE the process is the same. After assessing the crisis with other parents they accept their helplessness at this point and trust in the support of others to get them started in changing their behaviors.

The deep feelings that accompany this transition can seem almost overwhelming. We remember being in a local supermarket two days after our daughter's arrest, where we ran into a woman whose children had been our daughters' friends and who knew what was happening with us because her fifteen-year-old daughter was pregnant. She and Phyllis stood at their shopping carts crying while David walked away and other shoppers looked away.

Those feelings are what keep many of us from getting past our denial because they are too painful and frightening. Some parents come to a TOUGHLOVE group, do a crisis assessment one week, and don't return the next. Or perhaps they return to try to convince the group that there is some special circumstance surrounding their kid that the group doesn't understand.

As with us, one of the most difficult feelings people have is helplessness. Many families who have been struggling to "get a handle" on their kid's behavior get caught in this helplessness, often supported by ineffectual psychological counseling. The best way to help them get unstuck is to let them know that there is a solution. When other parents in the TOUGHLOVE group share their action-oriented success stories, these people begin to trust in the possibility of resolution and their helplessness dissipates.

TOUGHLOVE helps people get past their deep feelings by asking them to "take a stand." This involves making statements like "I will not allow my child to physically abuse me or any other family member," or "I will not allow my daughter to keep running away from home," or "I will not live with a stoned teenager." These stands are long-term goals and people cannot expect to reach them instantly.

Often people feel angry when they take a stand. Usually the stands they take are goals they have wanted for themselves and for their families for a long time but felt too powerless to achieve. The anger people feel at this time is different from the feelings they had when they stopped denial. The anger in taking a stand is more focused and with the TOUGHLOVE group's help can become "assertiveness," which directs energy and action and produces positive and productive changes.

In our own experience we found that without our heavy reliance on our friends we could easily have slipped back into old patterns. After our hurt and shock dissipated somewhat our guilt and fear made us forget the awful things our kid had done and we felt as if we were betraying her. Mary and Teresa kept us on the right track, holding to our stand, which was, "We will not have a daughter who is a criminal." We asked their advice at every turn, relying on them for the smallest transactions with our daughter, like getting her clothes to her, and for every communication with her. Parents who have been entangled in such unhealthy relationships with their children need someone else's explicit direction and hand-holding to help them begin anew.

This dependence is a phase that many parents hate and prefer to avoid at all costs, at least initially. Needing someone else is perceived in our culture as a sign of inadequacy and weakness that seems to contradict our pioneer spirit. In fact some individuals find the need to lean on someone else so threatening that they would prefer to go all the way back to denial again, but this retreat is usually just temporary. After all, what's at stake is the well-being of our families and our children, who are in danger of self-destruction if changes are not made.

It takes a strong person to ask for help. Being able to request assistance is *not* a sign of weakness, but a sign of strength and maturity. People need each other. We are not in this world alone and we don't have to act as if we are.

Like TOUGHLOVE groups who have helped members in many kinds of ways, we turned to friends for help with moving while our daughter was in jail and David was in the hospital with his broken ankle. With a pot of chili cooking on the stove, coworkers and friends packed up our belongings in one day, and what seemed an insurmountable task became a memorable event. The world need not seem like such a lonely place if we can learn to help each other.

TOUGHLOVE does not ask people to stay permanently dependent, rather to accept dependence as a temporary but essential circumstance. Parents begin by working out a "bottom line," with a plan and support. The bottom line is usually just for a week, a small step that a parent or a couple can agree upon and have a realistic chance of accomplishing. The smaller the step the better. People need to feel successful in making changes and a small, easily managed step is more useful than trying to resolve several years of difficulty all at once. The TOUGHLOVE group members help other parents keep to realistic goals.

Bottom lines are based on the stand that parents have taken. For us, with the stand "We will not have a daughter who is a criminal," the first steps included refusing to speak directly to our daughter on the telephone, refusing to put up bail money, and asking Mary and Teresa for advice on each decision.

One mother we knew resolved that she would not allow her daughter to be verbally abusive to her. Her TOUGHLOVE group members suggested that she change her usual pattern of scolding as her first bottom line. For instance, when her kid slammed the door upon returning home after school each day, Mom would invariably scold and her daughter would invariably scream invectives and storm out of the house until suppertime. Now Mom arranged to be talking on the telephone to a member of the group when her daughter came home and she ignored the slammed door. She reported at the next weekly TOUGHLOVE meeting that things were a little more peaceful at home and she was enjoying her daughter's puzzlement at her mom's new behavior.

Another dad reported how his wife didn't accept that their son was stealing from them. Instead she'd blame the neighbors. As his bottom line, Dad resolved to avoid mentioning his concern to his wife while other TOUGHLOVE moms invited his wife to a TOUGHLOVE meeting which she had previously refused to attend. Within two weeks she was a member of the TOUGH-LOVE group.

A twenty-five-year-old who was in the hospital with his second drug overdose found that his parents had decided not to visit him in the hospital. Instead other TOUGHLOVE parents came and informed him about drug rehabilitation facilities which were available to him. A few weeks later two of these parents drove him to the treatment facility he had chosen.

Sometimes small steps bring dramatic results, more often the process takes a while. Because our own daughter initially viewed her stay in jail as an "adventure," we were told by our support people to withhold assistance until she took a more realistic look at her difficult situation. When she did so we still kept our distance with new bottom lines like refusing to attend her trial, not allowing her to return home but insisting that she have a drug and alcohol evaluation, and ultimately that she complete some drug rehabilitation program. Each new bottom line evolved as previous ones were met with our daughter going through each phase while we received new advice and help from our support people.

Even though bottom lines are partial steps, not solving the whole problem by any means, they are still very difficult for parents. So the TOUGHLOVE group offers to support the parents in keeping their bottom line. A different group member might call each evening to see how they're doing, someone might actually come over to help directly. The support spurs parents on and transcends verbal support at the meeting with *active* support during the week between meetings. The support and the bottom line should be carefully planned and as specific as possible. If parents will call, they name the night they'll phone and exchange phone numbers immediately if a group phone list is not available. The more specific the plan, the more likely the bottom line's chance of success.

TOUGHLOVE group members must be careful not to get too zealous in their support. Parents must want the support that is offered. Like bottom lines that are foisted on people, unwanted support is frustrating to the recipient. Also group members must make it clear to the parents who are just beginning the process that it's O.K. to fail. The stigma of not completing a bottom line, even for several weeks in a row, should not keep parents from coming back. In fact, they should be encouraged to change the bottom line to something that they can really accomplish.

Many people resist support, especially if the bottom line seems very simple. They must be reminded that changes, however simple, represent a shift in patterns, a new way of being, and while they seem simple at the meeting, the next day the bottom line may look very different. Also, accepting support on little bottom lines makes it easier to accept support when "biggies" arrive. Phone calls between group members might be viewed as practice.

Early bottom lines may be just a commitment to come back to a second TOUGHLOVE meeting or promising to read other TOUGHLOVE materials. Parents can develop progressively stronger bottom lines until the impact of their actions begins to reach the heart of the matter, but for every family the pace and style may be different.

As parents make these small changes their confidence

returns and they find themselves feeling in charge of their own lives and families again. Being more in control they move toward independence.

We found ourselves growing stronger, David's leg was healing, and we were increasingly aware of our own limits. We refused to tolerate our daughters' "big mouths" and put limits on what we'd buy for whom and when. We began to see our children as people who needed to give in order to get and we established some detachment in dealing with their behavior.

David says that he struggled with the realization that to have our children we had to be willing to risk losing them. He feared the image of being a bad father and losing his family. Facing this fear was tough but necessary. Our friends supported him in this and let him know he was O.K. Without their help he could never have moved on with the changes he was making.

Independence occurs when parents are practicing the changes they have made with some ease. They may have fully accomplished one stand and be on their way to another, or they may be feeling very successful in working on their first stand. The process is still the same: setting bottom lines with a plan and support each week.

Independence is somewhat difficult to define clearly for it occurs in the minds of parents and is a matter of perception. Some people slip into independence with ease, some want it too quickly or get stuck in dependence. In any case the TOUGHLOVE group members work to help each other with the transition to independence.

One of the difficulties with this step is that many people see independence as the end of the process. Some families take what they need from others and forget to give something in return. Living in a world with other human beings means that complete independence doesn't really exist, for people need one another.

Ironically this false sense of independence is typical of troubled teenagers. Although they take their parents' support they perceive themselves as old enough and mature enough to be on their own, even though they are not. Their arrogance is often buoyed by artificial stimuli, alcohol, or other chemicals which create a false feeling of power. The need to give something back to their families is just not part of their reality.

The ultimate goal of TOUGHLOVE is to encourage parents to move beyond independence to interdependence: giving and getting. Every individual has his or her strengths and weaknesses. By giving assistance from our strengths and accepting help with our weaknesses the group as a whole becomes stronger than the sum total of its individuals.

TOUGHLOVE group members offer this kind of selective support to each other and by doing so move the group beyond independence. Parents feel their own crises recede and find the energy to help other parents. As the group matures to this state of interdependence there is a sense of mutual trust and good feelings that is a rarity in this dog eat dog world. We have rid ourselves of some of our snobbish notions since developing TOUGHLOVE. We always thought we had little in common with factory workers or old-fashioned conservatives or other people who didn't share our middle class, educated, white-collar values. But we realize now how much alike we all are in our suffering and that color, money, and education don't mean a thing when we help each other to revitalize our families and our communities.

TOUGHLOVE groups model the best of human social interaction: a cooperative community which serves the needs of both the individual and the group.

Interdependence is what families can achieve as well. A few weeks ago our daughter repeatedly mentioned how nice it was to feel we were friends and not just parents. What made her feel that way was her sharing and giving of her time, her resources, gifts, and help, her occasional assistance at the TOUGHLOVE office, her interest in us, and her openness about herself. She now values us beyond what we can give her and values what she has to offer us and what we take from her. On our behalf we can be frank with her, we enjoy her company, we like giving and taking from her. We like having her confidence and being valued. We are headed toward interdependence and so it goes with all three of our kids.

When a TOUGHLOVE group achieves some degree of interdependence the members begin to implement the last development phase: community involvement. The group members make a general, long-term commitment which extends beyond their immediate, personal crises to helping their community at large. The group develops a cooperative rapport with schools, police departments, the courts, social service agencies, clergy, and others who deal with troubled young people. Service clubs, businesses, and other groups with no direct relationship to the problem may also become involved in this community effort. When this occurs TOUGHLOVE group members will feel truly proud of their achievement, for they have created a valuable community service from the depths of their own despair, turning helplessness into positive action.

The process of change is a difficult odyssey. We have

attempted to ease the path by anticipating the dynamics of the process and providing carefully designed structures for TOUGHLOVE: crisis assessment, taking a stand, bottom lines, selective support, and community involvement. No one can eliminate the hardships that the traveler will face, but like the pioneers whose wagon trains made the trek across the American continent, we can improve our chances of success by working together in a spirit of cooperation and mutual support. We need not make the journey alone.

Chapter 14

Support Groups

"My wife, Gwen, and I decided to start a group. Gwen called around to all the churches and schools to see if we could get any help and we finally had our first meeting in our church. I kept calling other parents and a majority said, No, we are not having a problem. What I did was to have a form letter typed up and I copied it and I sent it to all those parents, saying even if you do not recognize the problem or you are not having a problem right now, this is my phone number. If you feel that you need information or you just want to talk, please call.

"We set a date for the parents to get together in the church. We had about thirty or forty people show up. That was due to Gus Booth, the principal of the alternative school. He contacted all the parents of the kids who went to the school. He really made a big effort. He could not be out in front because he felt that the parents would feel resentment toward him.

"We were so frightened and desperate. I just needed other people to lean on and I wanted other people to lean on me so that my hurt would not be as bad as it really was."

TOUGHLOVE parent/community support groups start in a wide variety of ways. Some are begun by parents who invite other troubled parents to their own home. These groups have been successful when they quickly obtain a community meeting place. Continuing to meet in someone's home encourages people to be too social and chatty, rather than task-oriented, and the group is not very productive. Problems with privacy can arise with the children of that household. Also a public meeting place is more accessible and provides a business-like atmosphere with room for the group to grow.

Sometimes a therapist, minister, policeman, or some other individual who works with troubled families fosters a group. Such people may be able to arrange the use of meeting space in their agency or establish liaison with other community resources or expedite the progress of the group in many ways, but the groups are most successful when the professional backs off soon and lets parents take responsibility for the group. If the professional stays parents tend to look to that individual for leadership, instead of trusting in their own ability to support each other, to brainstorm solutions, to find resources, and to manage the group.

Susan, the director of an alternative school, initiated one of the first TOUGHLOVE groups for parents of her students and found that she had to stop going to meetings to keep from interfering with the group. The group has been run exclusively by parents since her departure. Professionals can foster groups, but it is contrary to the fundamentals of TOUGHLOVE for professionals to run the groups. Such leadership hampers the group's effectiveness.

TOUGHLOVE groups meet once each week, usually on a weekday evening, every week of the year. Even if meeting nights fall on a holiday the group still meets, never missing a night. That way the group sustains its momentum and attendance. Although only a few parents may attend that holiday evening, everyone else knows that they missed a meeting. Groups which fail to meet every week find that regular attendance drops dramatically.

Most TOUGHLOVE groups do *not* pay rent for their meeting place. TOUGHLOVE parents help not only themselves but others, and a TOUGHLOVE group is a community service. In many instances agencies in a community offer free space because they want to be associated with TOUGHLOVE. Whatever funds the group raises, usually by collecting a small donation at each meeting, should not pay for rent but should be used to help the group's progress: for printing posters for publicity or sending representatives of the group for training.

TOUGHLOVE Weekend Workshops held in varied locations in the United States and Canada train parents and professionals to practice TOUGHLOVE effectively. Frequently members of existing groups that have not had training in TOUGHLOVE find themselves changing the structure of their meetings when they return to their groups after a Weekend Workshop.

The structure we suggest avoids leadership problems and keeps rambling to a minimum, while allowing for individual ideas and feelings to focus on developing action plans. We have found that the best way to accomplish this is to follow a structure which uses small subgroups of ten to twelve parents followed by sessions of the whole TOUGHLOVE group.

The meeting begins with small groups for "checking in," Most people feel closer and find it easier to talk in small groups, so the room is set up in circles of ten to twelve chairs. These small groups are most effective if they are comprised of parents who live near one another and can visit one another's homes when needed for support. Each small group appoints a leader to keep the group moving on the necessary tasks. The small groups open with parents sharing the last week's events. They specifically relate how their bottom line and their support for that bottom line worked during the week, what success they had and what difficulty.

This segment of the meeting lasts only thirty minutes, so there is not time for new bottom lines or lengthy discussion. The small-group leader watches the clock and keeps the discussion moving so that all members have a chance to "check in" during this portion of the meeting.

Some TOUGHLOVE groups may not be large enough to subdivide into the small groups, while other groups have so many newcomers at each meeting that they have to set up an orientation subgroup for them, facilitated by an older member who listens to them and explains what TOUGHLOVE is and how it works. Many TOUGHLOVE groups get stuck investing too much time with newcomers who don't even return for another meeting, while long-time members are pushed aside by the apparent urgency of the newcomers. Groups need to ask newcomers to observe the meeting, make a commitment to the group by coming back again and by reading from his book or other TOUGHLOVE materials which will help explain the TOUGHLOVE process to them.

The second segment is a general meeting when all the small groups join together into one large group with a coordinator keeping time and running the session. The coordinator begins by asking for "success stories" and group members report on any small or large accomplishment from the previous week. Applause helps everyone feel good about these positive steps and creates an encouraging and energizing atmosphere.

The rest of this forty-minute session is spent reviewing information from this book or other TOUGHLOVE materials, hearing guest speakers (lawyers, judges, doctors, agency people, police, school personnel), or discussing a practical task like the steps the group is taking to publicize itself to the community or learn more about the law. Remember to request that guest speakers observe the whole evening's meeting because they have much to learn from the TOUGHLOVE group. Avoid blame and blaming by stressing an attitude that asks, "How can we help each other?"

In the third segment of the meeting parents rearrange their chairs and return to their small groups. Parents now use the small group to set a new bottom line and to develop a specific plan and support for the new (and often scary) step they are about to take. The small-group leader has an obligation to see that every plan has offers of support from the group and that the group does not bully someone into making a bottom line that he or she is not really ready for. This session lasts forty minutes.

Finally parents return for a twenty-minute large group wrap-up. The coordinator asks parents to report *very briefly* on their bottom lines and support, with applause to encourage their determination. Some parents may need special support that they could not find in their small group, like someone to go to court with them.

Then the meeting comes to an official end. Many parents linger, however, to socialize or to meet with especially troubled individuals or to coordinate some business of the TOUGHLOVE group.

The meeting structure is small groups for thirty minutes, large group for forty minutes, small groups for forty minutes, large group for twenty minutes. Each segment of the structure has a specific purpose. Following this structure and approximate time-frame helps groups stay action-oriented and productive. Groups who do not use such a structure often deteriorate into coffee klatches and "bitch sessions" which achieve nothing.

Coordinators and other leadership roles in the organization should be rotated. Small-group leaders change as often as every week in some TOUGHLOVE groups, while large-group coordinators may serve for a few months. Dispersing the work of the organization into many hands keeps more people actively interested in the group and keeps especially hard-working individuals from "burning out" and quitting the group. Volunteering support, carrying out family negotiations, keeping track of the group's finances, putting up posters, visiting school guidance counselors to acquaint them with the group: all of these responsibilities can be shared among many willing people whose combined strength will move the TOUGHLOVE group into an active and favorable position in the community.

TOUGHLOVE parent support groups reach out to the community. Pairs of group members, called "action teams," visit schools, police departments, juvenile probation offices, and child welfare agencies to ask their cooperation. Always *nonblaming*, an action team asks for the individual's help, leaves reading material, and invites that person to attend a group meeting to see

A TOUGHLOVE PARENT SUPPORT GROUP

LEADERSHIP ROLES	DUTIES
TOUGHLOVE Coordinator	Maintains support structure: time, place, meeting format. Plans for information presentations or guest speakers. Central information source for available services. Coordinates with other TOUGHLOVE groups.
Small-group Leaders	Chairs small suport groups. Introduces new people. Moves group along and on track. Helps assess crises. Supportive confrontation. Helps set bottom lines. Identifies active support.
Public Relations Person	Responsible for posters, flyers, news media. Maintains contacts with schools, police, courts, service organizations.
Greeter	Welcomes new people. Runs orientation group. Ensures meeting room. Arranges for refreshments. Issues service contracts and maintains current telephone list.
Financial Wizard	Raises funds for refreshments, gas, telephone, bails, etc. Sells manuals. Administers other financial plans as agreed on by the group.

what TOUGHLOVE parents really do. Although some people do not respond favorably, at least at first, the TOUGHLOVE group members wear down skeptics with a consistently positive, cooperative attitude.

The public media, newspapers and radio and television stations, have proved to be sympathetic to TOUGH-LOVE. The openness of parents in discussing their family's situation, once they have stopped feeling guilty, disarms critics. Not only will the media cover the TOUGHLOVE group as a news story but most print and broadcast media will provide free public service announcements to publicize the weekly meetings. Some publications print the meeting time and place of the local TOUGHLOVE group every week because they consider it such an important community service.

Taking only minor precautions, like asking parents' permission to give their names to a reporter who wants to interview TOUGHLOVE families and requesting that the reporter not print names without permission, the TOUGHLOVE group can trust the media to provide an almost universally favorable response. In fact, after the group's debut in the local press, group members should expect invitations to send representatives to radio talk shows, parent-teacher associations, and service clubs, which all share a concern for "what's happening with kids today." Speaking only for their local group and not for the whole TOUGHLOVE movement and philosophy, parents need not be "experts." Candor and sincerity seem to make the best impression on an audience.

For a mature group, the best public relations tool seems to be having a guest or two at a meeting. When a group first gets organized visitors can detract from the meeting, but at later meetings parents will find that visitors are extremely impressed by the responsible, caring people they meet and by the no-nonsense, task-oriented focus of the meeting. A visit by a public official can begin a healthy and productive relationship. For instance a visiting county district attorney agreed to have his staff respond, in writing, to legal questions posed by a committee of TOUGHLOVE parents. The questions and answers were subsequently published cooperatively by several local TOUGHLOVE groups.

Other working relationships have developed. Juvenile probation officers feel free to contact group coordinators to check whether some parents who represent themselves as TOUGHLOVE parents were really involved with a local group. The local child welfare office makes arrangements through TOUGHLOVE parents for emergency housing for a teenager. When these kinds of relationships develop the TOUGHLOVE group is fulfilling its potential. Cooperation on the local level begins to replace the blame and bad feelings that usually prevail.

When TOUGHLOVE groups coordinate their activities with police, schools, courts, and county agencies, young people find the adult community unified and prepared to deal with them more effectively. They actually experience consequences for their negative actions. Truant teenagers are fined, not their parents. Drug abusing kids find themselves in rehabilitation programs because they know that their families and the authorities will not tolerate their behavior any longer. Runaways stop leaving home because they can no longer find sanctuary with their friends' parents.

The proliferation of TOUGHLOVE parent/community

support groups in the United States and Canada has proceeded at a surprisingly rapid pace. They seem to fill an urgent need for many parents and their accumulated impact will have a growing influence on the way our culture responds to its unruly young people.

Chapter 15

TOUGHLOVE
Is Tough

TOUGHLOVE is tough when your thirty-one-year-old son has recently returned to the mental institution for the fifth time in six years and you know you shouldn't see him, but a whining voice inside you says, "Oh, but it's Christmas. You can't abandon him, he'll be so alone and you don't want to be punishing."

But your support people from the TOUGHLOVE group tell you, "Yes, you do want to abandon that hurtful, rejecting, uncooperative, irresponsible, blaming child who just got himself committed hoping that you'll pick up the bill. That irresponsible child who held a job for over a year but at Thanksgiving chose to skip his medication, smoke dope, and launch himself into a rage. That rejecting child who lost his job because he would no longer do the work, thinking he was too good for everyone in the office, although other TOUGHLOVE parents helped him get the job in the first place when he was desperate for employment. That uncooperative child whose roommate finally asked him to leave because he played rock music all night and brought sleazy people to the apartment. That hurtful child who attempted a burglary. That blaming child who cited his mental illness as the cause and dumped the problem on his parents when the police caught up with him. He chose his actions and he chose to hospitalize himself and yes, you want him to know that you will no longer accept that kind of behavior."

TOUGHLOVE is tough when you're trying to be different with him. TOUGHLOVE is tough when you let the hospital know that you will *not* pay the bill and he has to seek state medical assistance. It's also tough when you know that his former co-workers refuse to feel sorry for him and they let him know clearly how disruptive he was and how awfully he treated everyone.

TOUGHLOVE is tough when you refuse to communicate with him and refer him to other TOUGHLOVE parents. He calmly reports to your stand-ins how comfortable he is in the institution and brags that he really was not responsible for his actions. He says that he is doing well at the hospital routine and that as soon as you stop "playing" with TOUGHLOVE, you'll be around to see him.

TOUGHLOVE is tough when you have to change. For six years this behavior has been going on, with thousands and thousands of dollars in hospitalization, psychiatrists, mopping up automobile accidents, and paying for new starts. You feel that you have to stop rescuing him but you are also afraid that if you do he'll commit suicide, or he'll be killed, or he'll stay in some back ward of the mental institution forever. Yet your actions for the past six years have only helped to sustain the tragedy and his destructive patterns.

For a while he functioned well but he ultimately got

tired of the ordinary and took his old path, playing out his fantasies, wishes, and desires, which were more important than his life, like an addict with a rock stardom fantasy but no guitar. Usually subservient to his every wish, you are now setting a new course in your relationship with him. And it's tough.

So now it's Christmas and he asks you to visit. But you don't. Instead you call your support people. "I don't want him to feel abandoned. I don't want to be punitive, that's not the point, is it?"

They understand your pain and they remind you, "The point of staying away, especially while he's hospitalized, is to *reject* that part of him that is 'sick' or acts 'sick.' If your son chooses to see you as punitive, so be it. Your son has punished you and others with his behavior. He needs to learn that he can't keep doing that to you, that he can't throw you away when he wants and yank you back again when he needs you."

"Yes, but he'll feel abandoned. I'm afraid he'll kill himself. I think we should visit for therapeutic reasons."

"But he's not abandoned. We'll call and visit him for you. You want him to know that you've abandoned that awful, irresponsible 'sick' part of him, that he'll have to be different and not play hospital whenever he likes. Now he says, 'Look what a good patient I'm being' for your approval. You are letting him know that he has to live a life outside of hospitals to get your attention.

"And yes, he could kill himself. But you can't protect him forever and play out the same old patterns again and again. Your son has strengths and he will have to use them now."

And then your TOUGHLOVE parents tell you something that is tough for them to say, that if you go to see him after making your commitment to stand firm, they will not be your support people anymore. You will have to find others in the group to support you. For if you visit him for sentimental reasons you will surely be in the same situation next Christmas. And so you sit tight and wait.

The frightening reality of some of the tough stances that we parents take is that our fears can come true. We perceive our acting-out children as so unpredictable that they might do anything. What we usually don't realize is that these acting-out children usually do their worst in our homes, under our protection, and exactly for that reason: they feel protected and feel they can get away with anything.

In our misguided thinking we reason, "At least I'm here and they're not killing themselves" or whatever fearful fantasy you have of the last ultimate horrible behavior. But what we do is keep them teetering on the edge of that dangerous precipice. They may fall over the edge even while we're watching. We can't save them, they must save themselves, and we need to allow them to choose and live with the choice. They may walk away from the precipice to safe ground or they may fall. If they fall they may climb back up or they may never return. However frightening the possibilities, we cannot really protect them.

And because most acting-out youth are abusing drugs and alcohol, we must put aside the logical and reasonable, which is tough to do. By altering their consciousness with drugs and alcohol our children can avoid recognizing their negative and unreasonable behavior. Their reality is distorted and reinforced not only by the physical substance but by their fellow abusers. Reason cannot penetrate the barrier that your children erect between you and them. Confrontation, with planning and support, is necessary.

TOUGHLOVE is tough when you must act differently than you ever have. When you must go to the police to turn in your kid. Or when you go to neighbors and friends to tell them about your child's outrageous behavior and ask their support. Or when you change what "good" and "bad" parenting always meant to you. Or when you ask school officials, police, social workers, and judges to help you control your own offspring. Or when you stand up in court and tell the judge you know your son is guilty. Or when you and your group take your kid to a detoxification center against her will. Or when you tell your daughter she cannot drive the family car because she is drunk. Or when you hear that your wayward daughter is back on barbiturates but you refuse to take her home without her going to a drug rehab. Or when you tell your oldest son he has to move out of the house. Or when your kid is living in a car and you avoid contacting him.

But TOUGHLOVE is loving. TOUGHLOVE is not nasty or abusive or vindictive. TOUGHLOVE means standing firm, knowing what plan to follow to deal with your kid's destructiveness, and loving your child enough to stop acting on wishes, hopes, and fantasies. TOUGHLOVE means loving your child enough to do what has to be done, no matter how hard you find the task.

When we refused to bail our daughter out of jail, it was the toughest thing we ever did. Just thinking about our child in jail was emotionally overwhelming. And it was Christmas and our memories of her as a child swept us like waves and bathed us in despair. We wept and wondered, but we held firm. Our fears obsessed us and it was no consolation to find out long afterward that the experience of Christmas in jail, according to our daughter, was not so bad. In fact it made us angry to think that we worried so. But our own doubts and fears are often more painful than reality itself and that's precisely what makes TOUGHLOVE so tough.

Chapter 16

Reconciliation

Seven months passed before we met with our renegade daughter. We had talked on the telephone and were told that she was doing all right in the rehabilitation center. Finally she asked to see us. We checked with our support people and they felt that a meeting at this time would be a good idea.

The meeting was arranged with a counselor and our whole family attended. We were nervous, apprehensive, and frightened of each other. In our hearts we were relieved to see our wayward kid but we also knew we would never feel quite the same way toward her: a way that excused her behavior and destructive manipulation. We now saw our daughter, not as the child of our emotions, but as a grown person who could hurt us and who had developed a whole other way of being that was alien to us. In that respect we barely knew her.

Our daugher was sure that we wouldn't forgive her and was relieved when the counselor helped her to see that she could earn our forgiveness. Although this first meeting was difficult and strained, we had several more meetings while our daughter was at the rehab and we all began to loosen up. With the counselor's help we decided that she could not live in our home for now, but that we could gradually build a new relationship.

Like us, other TOUGHLOVE families also reach the point after the "crisis" when their son or daughter says, "I want to be part of this family." It's a good faith move and the TOUGHLOVE support network is very important in helping the family deal with their child. Support people guide the family in establishing limits and actions because emotions can cloud parents' vision again.

Parents have drawn the line and said, "I will not live with you the way you have been," and now their child is saying, "O.K." and listening to the steps he or she needs to take to return to the family. At such an emotional time some group members may help take over parental decisions.

The TOUGHLOVE group members who agreed to work with the family are temporary family authorities, providing selective support to maintain bottom lines and to protect the family from nonproductive behavior like old arguments and endless blame. The first family meetings are concerned with setting plans for cooperative living for only a short period of time, a day or two, a week at most. Often group members have already met with the kid and have established guidelines, contacted the youth's school, or made an appointment for a drug and alcohol evaluation.

TOUGHLOVE parents do not meet with young people who come to the meeting high, who act belligerent, or who seem to agree to virtually anything. These are signs of bad faith and are unacceptable. The young person is asked to call for another meeting when he or she is ready to act in good faith.

TOUGHLOVE selectively supports parents and their

children in keeping to bottom lines. Most parents have already changed their behavior and now their kids are asked to do the same. The TOUGHLOVE support people gently push and prod families toward jointly making decisions and setting new bottom lines.

Even though all of us hope we can arrange a cooperative way of living with each other, in these TOUGHLOVE family meetings we must accept that a disruptive young person may not agree to back down and accept his or her dependence on parents. Whatever the outcome, TOUGHLOVE members are supportive to both parents and children, letting a kid know that he or she can stay at one of their homes for a brief period until another meeting or arrangement can be made. TOUGH-LOVE members also support parents in accepting what's happened and encourage them to "hang tough" if necessary. While the meetings can take place again and again, TOUGHLOVE support people must remember that they are *not* responsible for a "happy" ending. The ending, sad or happy, is up to the family.

Once the family has worked through the first tenuous days and weeks, the process of reconciliation begins: a process which involves the acceptance of our pain and coming to terms with our guilt. The guilt we parents feel is from our actions in the past and from the pain of what has happened to our family. There is a great deal to resolve. Reconciling how we are going to live with or without our child. Coming to terms with our hopes, dreams, and feelings. Deciding which pieces belong to us and which pieces belong to our child.

Reconciliation involves accepting the reality of who our kid is right now and deciding how we will interact with him or her. Not trusting until trust is earned.

Not being fooled by manipulations. Setting our own limits an sticking to them. Recognizing our kid and not imposing the unreality of a kid we wish we had.

We may feel frustrated and incomplete because we cannot get our child to what we consider a safe place: a high school diploma, a college degree, a marriage, or whatever our own dream was. We feel stymied and cut off in midair. But we must recognize that our child has said with his or her behavior, "You can't be who you want to be with me." The TOUGHLOVE group helps us manage that painful rejection and learn different ways to be a parent to our child.

Reconciliation means you are no longer willing to be managed by your kid's manipulations.

You can't be manipulated by your kid when you:

- set your own limits and stick to them.
- keep in touch with schools, counselors, and TOUGH-LOVE group members.
- stop needing to trust your kid.
- check out how you are responding to your kid with others who know you and your situation.
- accept and recognize how your kid has manipulated you.
- rid yourself of false parental pride.
- have self-acceptance rather than self-hate.

The road hasn't been smooth since our most troubled years. One daughter struggled with her street values about men—"I have to have a man, I'm nothing without one"—while another feared living on her own after college. There were times when drug and alcohol abuse drove us away and times of saying, "I will not be there for you or with you when you cheat, lie, and abuse drugs."

We have been suckers and patsies many different times, supplying funds for rent or a coat or some other necessity, not realizing that the money really goes to sustain a lifestyle of which we don't approve, friends who don't work, or a drug dependency. We have been hooked, manipulated, and conned by our children, although less through the years as our kids have become people we like. When one of our daughters now says that we should stop giving, it's enough and it makes her greedy, we back off realizing that she has made important changes in her behavior and in her relationship with us.

Our children come and go in our life right now. One is getting her bearings again, saving money and deciding what her next step will be. She lives with us and we enjoy sharing our living space and life space with her.

Our children have found meaning on different paths. One sought marriage and family and likes the feeling of responsibility in having children, another finds a career rewarding and a more serious relationship with a man both important and difficult. A third found working in a store worthwhile for a long time and grew up there among caring adults who were like family to her.

Our immediate family all live within an hour's drive of each other and the closeness is nice when times are good and when we are supportive of each other. When things are hard for one or another of us, we get enmeshed in the issues. Phyllis gets angry, David withdraws, and the kids choose sides and argue. Then it's not so pleasant and we feel like moving. We have no idea how long we'll live close by, but we know how important our children are to us. And even when there's friction, we have our limits and have stopped interacting in hurtful and hurting ways.

Two years ago we passed the responsibility for keeping our family history to our daughters. For Christmas we gave each of them a family album of her own with complete history, family recipes, pictures, an audio tape with explanations, birth and marriage dates, and a written series of anecdotes about our family. As we prepared the albums we recapitulated our family experience. Our daughters cried when we presented the finished product on Christmas Eve and it was apparent that night that we had narrowed the distances among ourselves, for everyone shared the chores, supported each other, and even played games together. Since then each daughter has added to her own album, symbolically and literally sharing in the responsibility for our family and who we are.

Part IV

THE TOUGHLOVE SOLUTION

Chapter 17

Conclusion

At the heart of the TOUGHLOVE solution is a cooperative community. If young people in our communities are in touble, then our communities themselves are in trouble. The problem belongs to all of us. All of our families in all of our communities throughout North America are experiencing unacceptable behavior from a growing number of our young people.

We need to get together to support the goal of TOUGHLOVE: people living together in a caring way. Our families and communities need to respond correctively to outrageous adolescent behavior. Mutual support and shared responsibility are fundamental to the process. For ultimately we do not have "your" children and "my" children but "our" children. Not only parents, but teachers, police, caseworkers, clergy, probation officers, therapists, judges, and citizens supporting a coordinated effort to change the hurtful environment in our communities.

The choice is ours: to continue blaming parents, schools, drug pushers, police, Dr. Spock, and other favorite targets or to change our responses to the problem. We can make that choice right now.

In communities from coast to coast people have decided to change their responses to the problem. No longer blaming or accepting blame, they establish support groups for parents, develop communication between local agencies and individuals, and coordinate their community's responses to truancy, drug abuse, running away, vandalism, theft, and violence so that young offenders experience real consequences and receive appropriate assistance in changing their behavior.

The TOUGHLOVE solution is not utopian. The changes among young people that need to occur will not be easy or sudden. Drug abuse and unacceptable behavior will not disappear. But the frustration of those adults who deal with troublesome youth can be eased by the cooperative environment which TOUGHLOVE encourages and the real sense of progress that prevails in a TOUGHLOVE community.

TOUGHLOVE is a solution to the problem of unacceptable behavior among young people. Psychological solutions often do not work. Searching for the causes of negative behavior does not necessarily make it stop and instead can prolong it. Supporting parents, encouraging cooperation in the adult community, and making acting-out young people accountable for their behavior comprise the fundamental activities of TOUGHLOVE and they are essential to any meaningful improvement in our current dilemma: What do we do about kids today?

TOUGHLOVE helps parents understand what's happening to them and their family and what to do about it. By revealing our own painful experiences to other parents, by admitting our mistakes, by recognizing our culture's pervasive influence on us and our children, we help other parents relax and face their own situation. They realize that the cause and cure of their kid's problems do not solely reside in parents, but in the whole community.

TOUGHLOVE fosters community and mutual support. By reducing the extreme competition and improving the communication among agencies and individuals, we model non-blaming, cooperative behavior. Both parents and cooperating professionals are buoyed by the positive results.

TOUGHLOVE empowers people. Parents learn the skills, attitudes, and strategies that enable them to change their own lives. We reduce our dependence on experts by helping each other. We avoid professional counselors and therapists who blame parents. We patronize those therapists who encourage young people to take responsibility for their own behavior and to recognize their dependence on and obligation to their families.

TOUGHLOVE modifies demands for intense personal relationships among family members and extends relationships to other adults and young people in their communities. By involving other people in our families we also reduce the isolation of the nuclear family, torn loose from the traditional three-generation family or old fashion neighborhood supports. The TOUGHLOVE parent/community support group fulfills functions often performed by nearby family and neighbors in communities of yesteryear.

TOUGHLOVE also modifies our excessively idealistic view of what a parent *should* be. "Great expectations lead to little results." We are attempting to live by ideal views of parent, mate, and family and we feel disappointment or failure when we don't reach the ideal. We feel victimized. TOUGHLOVE readjusts our cultural expectation for our families to a more realistic plane. "The Brady Bunch" and "Father Knows Best" were only TV shows, after all.

We cannot achieve perfection. Trying to do so will make us crazy. Nor do we have to accept horrible behavior. We don't have to sigh and hope it will pass or wish for bygone days. We can stop it by taking action here and now.

In a different time or place the TOUGHLOVE solution would not be appropriate. Or necessary. But for our present situation the difficult steps that parents and communities must take in responding correctively to their unruly teenagers are exactly as TOUGHLOVE prescribes. We say that because we know the process works. Time and time again parents have regained their self-confidence, cooperative brothers and sisters have regained their parents' attention, and the acting-out children have made choices about how to live. Most choose to meet their family's demands and change for the better, some do not. But the crisis becomes their own, not their family's, and they themselves must live with the implications of their choices.

And that's the best that we can do. Bring about resolution for ourselves and our families. The TOUGHLOVE solution involves risks. But so does doing nothing. We can't force our wayward children to change. That is their decision. But we can show them TOUGHLOVE. That is our decision.

Appendix

FAMILIES

Thousands of families have practiced TOUGHLOVE with their unruly children since we established the first parent/community support group in New Hope, Pennsylvania, in 1978. The following interviews with TOUGH-LOVE families were selected from among a large number of interviews conducted by Daurelle Golden. They represent a wide variety of circumstances and their experiences should enhance the reader's understanding of TOUGHLOVE, not only from the parents' point of view but from that of young people whose behavior brought their parents to TOUGHLOVE. The interviews are largely verbatim, with details and names changed.

Our first family, the Bergers, came to TOUGHLOVE for support after they had confronted their son's problem. They joined the group to heal their wounded parental pride by helping others. We feel their son is accurate when he says they are no longer so arrogant. Like many of us they learned that they need others and so they remain open and take direction. Perhaps their son Neal could use a little humility himself.

169

INTERVIEWER: Why did you seek TOUGHLOVE out?

MOM: Because my son was having problems with marijuana.

INTERVIEWER: What kind of problems were you encountering?

MOM: He had cashed in his whole bank account, which consisted of about $670. . . . dealing until I found the bankbook with no money in it. He had stolen from my husband's stamp collection. I felt that I really had to do something about it. This was the second time that he had turned to pot and I knew that he wasn't coping with his problems. And I really didn't know what to do about it.

INTERVIEWER: You heard about TOUGHLOVE through...?

MOM: I didn't know what to do about the problem at all. My brother had had a problem with his child and he had used a rehab in Philadelphia, successfully. I called him and he had just seen a TV program with the Yorks. The Yorks were his counselors at the rehab. That was before they got started in TOUGHLOVE. So he suggested that I call there. When I did they had given me the name of Alice Murphy, who was heading TOUGHLOVE here in Mifflin.

INTERVIEWER: Who just happened to live around the corner at that point?

MOM: Yeah. We didn't even know it then. She told us the experience she had had with her daughter. We knew that we wanted residential placement. I felt that if he had to work out his problems, he had to be away from home, away from his friends, otherwise it would not be successful. She told me about the rehab that her daughter was in and how much she liked it and how successful her daughter was. So we had the same rehab. In fact it took us three days, he was in the rehab home, and the first day we put him in the home, we went to our first TOUGHLOVE meeting.

INTERVIEWER: Had you sought any help previously?

MOM: For years. With psychologists, psychiatrists, testing, everything.

INTERVIEWER: Social service agencies? Did you go to Family Services?

MOM: No, just privately on our own. He was difficult to handle. He was a behavior problem since the age of two.

INTERVIEWER: What kind of experience did you have with other places?

MOM: Not so good. They all said, Well, treat him differently. Be easier with him. Don't expect too much from him.

INTERVIEWER: Basically, it was *you* who had to do something different?

DAD: We had to make adjustments to him rather than him making adjustments to us.

INTERVIEWER: How did that feel?

DAD: Pretty good until we found out that it didn't work anyway.

MOM: I really believed it, I thought, well, maybe I'm too hard on him. I really shouldn't be. There were a lot of parents who always criticized me for being too hard on my children. On all of them. Well, maybe it was me, I thought. It only got worse and worse as each year went by. I was really at my wits' end. He had to go out and be a productive entity and a responsible one because I'm not going to be here forever. To be with him and protect him.

INTERVIEWER: How long were you with TOUGHLOVE?

DAD: Since March of 1981.

INTERVIEWER: And you are still involved with it now, you still go to the meetings?

MOM: Yes.

INTERVIEWER: Why did you stay with it?

MOM: There were people there who helped me when I needed help and I felt that I should give some of that back. It really aids us in the end. It keeps us strong because we have a younger child and it reminds me constantly that you have to be strong.

INTERVIEWER: When you got involved with TOUGH-LOVE, what was the hardest thing for you to accept about TOUGHLOVE?

MOM: At Passover time my son was in the rehab. Passover is the family meal, certain rituals that go on, and it was always very important and I asked Phyllis York if we could go up and have dinner with him. And she said no. That was hard for me.

DAD: The hardest was learning to be consistently tough. That was a tough part.

INTERVIEWER: Saying no over and over again . . . ?

DAD: Saying no and conditioning yourself as to what had to be done and understanding the process. Understanding your own shortcomings and weaknesses.

INTERVIEWER: That was the hardest to accept and also the most difficult for you to do?

MOM: Yeah.

INTERVIEWER: How did you handle that? Did you receive any support?

MOM: We received a tremendous amount of support. People came over after the meeting and said, Don't worry, it will be all right. You'll get over it.

INTERVIEWER: What did you hope to get from TOUGH-LOVE?

MOM: A child that I always wanted. A child that would be responsible, not to worry about.

DAD: Relief.

INTERVIEWER: And did you get that?

MOM: Yes.

INTERVIEWER: What rewards did you get?

MOM: My own son. You feel like you are getting the child back again after they have been on drugs. You feel that he is not lost to you. That's wonderful. Knowing that you are helping to clean up the neighborhood. Just educating other parents.

INTERVIEWER: What risks did you take?

MOM: I really didn't have to take any risks.

DAD: You run the risk of being shamed by your associates, by your friends. Unless they understand the problems themselves, they tend to pooh-pooh what you are doing. You are not strong enough to know your own kid. That's the real risk that you run.

MOM: That you are a terrible mother. That you are putting your kid in a rehab home.

INTERVIEWER: So would you say that it was a risk putting him in a rehab home?

MOM: Socially. If your child doesn't want to go and runs away, you lose the child altogether.

INTERVIEWER: So you feel that it was worth whatever risks you did take? What kind of support did you get from people during this time? What kinds of things did people do for you?

MOM: I always had difficulty knowing exactly what to do or say in a particular situation. My husband didn't but I did. I would call my brother, who was really a trained professional counselor. I was calling TOUGHLOVE members and asking them. Instead of saying something general, they would be specific. I would take their advice. Say it almost word for word. Or did the act exactly and it worked out for me. The psychologists were talking theoretically.

INTERVIEWER: You needed action.

MOM: I needed specifics.

INTERVIEWER: And did you do the same things for other people?

MOM: Yes. We have people over to our house all the time.

INTERVIEWER: What were your relatives' reactions to what you were doing? Did you get support? Did you have any nonsupportive people?

DAD: We had friends who kind of backed off very quickly.

INTERVIEWER: But no relatives. In other words no grandparents. How did they feel?

MOM: They were all for it. It was our friends who backed off. They felt that they would protect their child even if the child had killed someone purposely.

INTERVIEWER: So your family supported what you were doing?

MOM: All of my family did, yes.

DAD: But it really didn't matter, because we were not looking for support.

INTERVIEWER: It helps to have it though.

DAD: Yes. We had our support group who were helping us.

MOM: We met with our TOUGHLOVE support group once or twice a week. And that was really helpful.

INTERVIEWER: How do you feel about the community aspects of TOUGHLOVE?

DAD: Ideally or practically?

INTERVIEWER: Both. What were your experiences?

DAD: Ideally, you hope that the community will support you and practically you find very little support. People don't care, they don't want to get involved.

INTERVIEWER: How about the police, for instance?

DAD: It's been slow, but they have been turning around. They do give us some support. As a force it's probably average.

INTERVIEWER: How about the schools?

DAD: The schools still do not understand our program. They have not made the effort to participate in TOUGHLOVE. Individuals, however, are beginning to understand more and are supporting us. But basically, the community at large is not really into TOUGHLOVE.

MOM: I found the little things exciting. I had a school principal suggest a family to us. A probation officer. Individually.

INTERVIEWER: Any social service agencies? Have you had to deal with any of those?

MOM: They are very helpful.

INTERVIEWER: So do you feel friendlier toward the community, do you feel you understand the community better?

MOM: Yes.

INTERVIEWER: Do you feel that you have more supportive people around you now?

DAD: We have a network of supportive people. A very close-knit group of people and it doesn't expand beyond that. It really amounts to our immediate family here and just the TOUGHLOVE people. They are the only people we can draw support from.

INTERVIEWER: Have you made new friends through TOUGHLOVE?

MOM: Oh yes.

INTERVIEWER: Do you recommend TOUGHLOVE?

MOM: Absolutely.

DAD: Only for those who are willing to help themselves. My feeling is that if they are using it as a social environment, I'd rather not see the people come.

INTERVIEW WITH SON NEAL

INTERVIEWER: Neal, how did you feel about TOUGH-LOVE at the beginning?

NEAL: I didn't care. I didn't know. All I knew was that I was doing rehab and that was it.

INTERVIEWER: Did you have any idea what it was all about?

NEAL: Not really. They would try and tell me.

INTERVIEWER: But you did not listen.

NEAL: No.

INTERVIEWER: Do you feel that TOUGHLOVE was helpful to you at all?

NEAL: In some areas yes, in some areas no.

INTERVIEWER: What areas?

NEAL: I do believe that in TOUGHLOVE some of the things are correct but some of their opinions conflict with my opinions.

INTERVIEWER: For instance?

NEAL: Trying to make the kid conform against his will. Sometimes it just won't work. You take the risk of the kid just splitting on you or there are many other things. I just can't really explain. If the kid is going to conform, I would say yes. That's when TOUGHLOVE comes in. But if he isn't you are just beating your heads against the wall. It doesn't do any good for you or the kid.

INTERVIEWER: Do you feel that TOUGHLOVE hindered you at all?

NEAL: No.

INTERVIEWER: How did TOUGHLOVE change your parents?

NEAL: When I went into rehab, they were the most confused, they were the most upset, inconsistent, and sometimes arrogant people I ever knew. At least through my eyes that is the way it appeared. Upon my exit, they got a lot of things together which I never thought they would. They were consistent in what they said, they weren't so confused, and not arrogant.

INTERVIEWER: Did they give you any surprises?

NEAL: Some surprises like rules that had to be followed now, consequences, and I had never seen that before. That blew my mind.

INTERVIEWER: How do you feel about TOUGHLOVE now?

NEAL: Some of the time I could go in there and tell them a couple of things and other times they could probably come in and tell me a few things.

INTERVIEWER: Give me an example?

NEAL: Throwing the kid out of the house. Sometimes it's good. It all depends on the situation. Charging your kid with incorrigibilities. If it's going to do any good, do it. You have to take the whole situation, get all the data. Then make your decision. I'm not saying that TOUGHLOVE doesn't do that.

INTERVIEWER: Do you feel that you understand what they are talking about?

NEAL: If I don't understand, they usually explain it to me. If I ask. But sometimes they can't.

INTERVIEWER: How come you haven't gone to any meetings?

NEAL: I have never been invited.

INTERVIEWER: Would you like to go?

NEAL: I would like to see what they do in there. From what I hear, they sit down and say, Well, this is the bottom line for this week. If they have a problem they talk about it.

INTERVIEWER: So you would be curious to find out what they really do?

NEAL: I would like them to invite me to their meetings.

The Benson family is not extremely verbal and our interviewer works hard. Daughter Ruth is particularly noncommunicative, which may be related to the presence of her friend Stacy. Stacy, on the other hand, acts as Ruth's alter ego, talking for her, so we included an interview with her.

Like all the families, the Bensons value support. This family's generosity now stretches beyond their children's demands to the community at large. Their support for others leaves less room for indulgence of their daughter.

INTERVIEWER: How many children do you have?
MOM: Two.
INTERVIEWER: What are their ages?
MOM: Fourteen and eighteen.
INTERVIEWER: Why did you seek out TOUGHLOVE?
MOM: We were having difficulty with my daughter, Ruth. We had been to psychiatrists, psychologists, without any help.
INTERVIEWER: What was the difficulty?
MOM: Drugs.
INTERVIEWER: What was her behavior like?
MOM: Off the wall.

INTERVIEWER: What kinds of things did she do?

MOM: Terrible language, temper tantrums, unruly, unmanageable.

INTERVIEWER: How about school?

MOM: Flunking everything.

INTERVIEWER: How about curfew?

MOM: That she always adhered to. That was the one thing that she did do.

INTERVIEWER: Did she resort to any physical violence?

MOM: She came in high twice. She picked the drawers out of her dresser and threw them. She weighs eighty pounds and I could not handle her.

INTERVIEWER: The help that you sought, what was that like?

MOM: We would force her to go, half the time she wouldn't go. When she would go, I would have to go with her. I would do it because I was desperate. And I would do all the talking.

INTERVIEWER: What kinds of things did they tell you?

MOM: That she was not a drug addict. That she did not have a drug problem.

INTERVIEWER: What did they attribute it to?

MOM: She has very bad eyesight. They attributed it to that. Bad behavior to her eyesight. She was small and she saw everything little. When she finally wore glasses, then things got big. And that was the psychological problem.

INTERVIEWER: Did they give you any advice or solutions, or what to do?

MOM: Nothing, just talk.

INTERVIEWER: How did that make you feel?

MOM: Horrible.

INTERVIEWER: How long a period was this going on?

MOM: About a year.

INTERVIEWER: How long have you been with TOUGH-LOVE? How did you find out about TOUGHLOVE? What brought you to it?

MOM: A friend of mine's child had been at this program and they knew about the Yorks. We were out one night and met them and their son was friendly with my daughter. They asked if we would be interested in forming a group with them. And we were desperate. We tried everything and that is how we met the Yorks.

INTERVIEWER: And how long have you been involved with TOUGHLOVE?

MOM: About a year and a half.

INTERVIEWER: Why did you stay with it?

MOM: To help other people.

INTERVIEWER: What kinds of changes did it make for you?

MOM: In my home?

INTERVIEWER: Yes. When you first got involved, what was the hardest thing to accept about TOUGHLOVE?

MOM: Nothing. They told us that we had to change our behavior and I am a very hyper person. My husband is a very quiet person. And switching roles was very tough.

INTERVIEWER: So you would say that was the most difficult thing for you to do as well as to accept?

MOM: Yes. The other difficult thing was when my daughter chose to leave. That week was probably the hardest week of my life.

INTERVIEWER: What happened with that, what did she do?

MOM: She came in high one day and we took her to the Yorks. They were doing private therapy at that time. She had a temper tantrum and David sat on her and had my husband physically handle her. They told us to leave and that she could stay there. We left and she ran away. The police called us to come get her, that she was not a resident of the community, and that they couldn't handle her. We said that, no, we would not, that she had a place to live and she was a resident. I guess from ten in the morning until twelve P.M. she was out on her own. She decided that she would go back to the Yorks. Wondering where she was was difficult.

INTERVIEWER: And throughout this whole time you were in touch with the Yorks?

MOM: Constantly.

INTERVIEWER: Did they tell you how to deal with the police when they called?

MOM: A friend of theirs, who was a lawyer who was in TOUGHLOVE, was giving us support.

INTERVIEWER: So you all knew ahead of time how you would deal with it?

MOM: Yes. They wouldn't let me give in.

INTERVIEWER: What did that feel like?

MOM: Horrible. It felt terrible. You have to understand that she was a very spoiled child to begin with. Overindulged. Over everything.

INTERVIEWER: So it was hard for you to handle?

MOM: Yes. Then she slept at the Yorks' and they had a meeting with her. They called us and said that she was ready to come home. We drove up there and picked her up. On the way home, she started to act out. When we got home, she hadn't eaten in two days, she went into the closet and took out a candy bar and dropped it on the floor. My husband said to her, "Pick it up." She said, "I'm not picking up that fucking candy bar." He said, "Pick it up or you get out." He picked her up bodily and put her on the doorstep and locked the door. She was gone for a week.

INTERVIEWER: She was on her own territory now, so she had a place to go?

MOM: Right. She stayed at a friend's house. A TOUGHLOVE parent and they knew how to handle her.

INTERVIEWER: Had you given her the name or the place?

MOM: No, not at that point, we just put her out and she is not a street person.

INTERVIEWER: What was it like when she was out of the house? How did you feel?

MOM: I felt terrible. She called us about every hour and I just hung up the phone.

INTERVIEWER: What were her calls about?

MOM: To come back to the house. She loved us. She sent us a letter about how much she loved us. And all the things that had happened in the family were her fault and how sorry she was for it. She called my sister, who is like her grandmother, and said to my sister, "Did they turn you also against me?" My sister called me hysterically crying. "You'll just have to trust us. If you love me, just do what I say," I told her. She did.

INTERVIEWER: Did she cooperate?

MOM: Yes.

INTERVIEWER: How about other relatives, did they cooperate?

MOM: No one else knew. My mother-in-law knew, but she was in Florida. Friends of mine were fantastic.

INTERVIEWER: She was out for this week, what were the circumstances that surrounded her coming back home? Did she come home after that?

MOM: Yes. We told her that she had to go for help. She had to abide by our rules. We had a meeting. The Yorks chose someone that they thought would be good for her. She went to see the young lady twice before she could come back to the house.

INTERVIEWER: Was it a counselor?

MOM: Yes. A drug therapist.

INTERVIEWER: How old was Ruth at the time all of this was going on?

MOM: Sixteen. It started at sixteen.

DAD: The first negotiaton was with the Yorks. The second time she was out about a week.

INTERVIEWER: That was when she was with another TOUGHLOVE parent?

DAD: The parent was not really a TOUGHLOVE parent. She just went over there.

INTERVIEWER: These other people, were they good friends of yours?

DAD: No, we just knew them.

INTERVIEWER: But you are saying that they cooperated?

DAD: Yes.

INTERVIEWER: What was her behavior like when she was there?

DAD: The model child. Beautiful. She called us every day. She wrote us a letter. She wrote a three-page letter asking to come home.

MOM: How much she loved everybody and how she tore the family apart.

INTERVIEWER: She agreed to go to counseling?

DAD: That was one of the parts of the negotiation.

INTERVIEWER: What were some of the other things?

MOM: Curfew.

DAD: No temper tantrums.

MOM: No foul language. She had to be responsible for her own behavior.

DAD: There were just about three or four different things.

MOM: No drugs.

INTERVIEWER: When you brought her home, how were things?

DAD: Very quiet. She wasn't good or bad. She was just there.

INTERVIEWER: Did she test at all?

MOM: No, she didn't test at all.

INTERVIEWER: And she went to counseling once a week?

MOM: Twice a week.

INTERVIEWER: Was this during a school year?

MOM: No, it was summer.

INTERVIEWER: So she had part of the summer to stay here?

DAD: It was in August when it happened.

INTERVIEWER: Then did she go back to school?

MOM: Yes.

INTERVIEWER: How have things been since?

MOM: Things have been great. Her marks have gone up.

DAD: Progressively better.

MOM: She's looking at the colleges now. It's just gotten better all along.

INTERVIEWER: Is she in school now?

MOM: Yes. She had to repeat a year.

INTERVIEWER: So she is being a lot more responsible for herself?

MOM: Yes.

INTERVIEWER: When you first got involved with TOUGH-LOVE, what did you hope to get from it?

DAD: We were going for anything or anybody that could help us. We didn't know anything about TOUGHLOVE.

MOM: We really didn't know what we wanted to get from it but we knew that we wanted a change in our house.

INTERVIEWER: And did you get it?

MOM: Yes.

INTERVIEWER: What rewards would you say that you have gotten?

DAD: Much more respect. A lot more communication.

MOM: She's pleasant to be with.

DAD: Definitely more love. She wants to be with us now.

INTERVIEWER: Would you say that you took any risks?

MOM: I think we took a big risk when she was out of the house.

DAD: I don't think so. Talking about it now it was not a risk but at the time, it was.

MOM: She was a little girl and could have become a street person.

DAD: I think some of these drug kids are dependent upon their families and once that prop is taken out from under them, they panic as well.

INTERVIEWER: So you feel that the risks that you took were worth it?

MOM: Well worth it.

INTERVIEWER: How did the Yorks show you how to change? What were some of the specific things that they wanted you to change?

MOM: That I had to take the back seat and my husband had to become more aggressive. That we had to make her responsible for her own behavior.

DAD: They waited till we acted on something and they stopped us and said, No, do it the other way.

INTERVIEWER: Was Ruth there at the time?

MOM: We would go to family sessions also with the Yorks. Twice a week. There were a lot of parents from TOUGHLOVE that were here to support us. They did everything that we couldn't do.

INTERVIEWER: Which was?

MOM: Dealing with the police.

DAD: We were doing that but they were just backing us up all the way.

MOM: You were much stronger through that time than I was.

INTERVIEWER: That was a change, allowing him to take the front seat?

MOM: Yes.

INTERVIEWER: How were friends that were not TOUGH-LOVE-related, did they support you through this period?

MOM: Yes.

INTERVIEWER: So you did not have any interference?

MOM: No.

INTERVIEWER: How do you feel about the community aspects of TOUGHLOVE? What can

TOUGHLOVE contribute to a community? What kinds of support have you given to other families?

MOM: Like going to court, going to negotiation sessions. Children in my home.

INTERVIEWER: Have you gotten to know the police through your situation?

DAD: Yeah.

MOM: He has but I have not.

INTERVIEWER: How did they respond to TOUGHLOVE?

DAD: Well, the Youth Juvenile Officer doesn't want to sit and learn about it. But the other police are a little bit more assenting than he is.

INTERVIEWER: How about the schools?

DAD: The superintendent of the schools was at one of the meetings and he made a comment that what we should do is get more publicity out that TOUGHLOVE isn't just for people who throw their kids out. That's the image that TOUGHLOVE has. He would recommend people to come to TOUGHLOVE.

INTERVIEWER: How about any social service agencies?

DAD: The girls have been going to them so they know more about that than I do. The County Court Juvenile Judge was at one of our meetings and he brought the whole staff of social workers.

MOM: They have been very helpful.

INTERVIEWER: What kinds of ways have they helped?

DAD: Whenever we needed anything we could just call them and they would help. The social services changed completely after that meeting. They had been very hardnosed about TOUGHLOVE. They turned around a hundred and eighty degrees.

INTERVIEWER: Do you feel friendlier to these parts of the community now? Do you feel like you understand them better?

MOM: Oh yes, definitely. Before we never had any dealings with them. My daughter never had any dealings with the police so we never had any dealings with them.

INTERVIEWER: Do you feel that you have more supportive people around you now?

MOM: Oh definitely.

DAD: We must have been involved in at least ten or fifteen cases.

INTERVIEWER: In a year...?

MOM: In a year and a half. We are always called.

INTERVIEWER: So you are very active?

MOM: Yes. Very active.

INTERVIEWER: Have you made new friends?

MOM: Yes. Some very close friends.

INTERVIEWER: How do you think that came about?

MOM: Through the support. You become very close when people are giving you support.

INTERVIEWER: I guess you have something in common.

DAD: Ruth is willing to help with another child if that child is in trouble. I don't know whether she would say at this point how much good TOUGHLOVE did her but I think she's at the point where she'd say it didn't hurt her. She doesn't say anything negative about TOUGHLOVE, she doesn't say anything positive either.

MOM: She says one of the greatest things that happened to her was her encounter with the Yorks.

INTERVIEWER: Would you recommend TOUGHLOVE?

MOM: Definitely.

INTERVIEW WITH DAUGHTER RUTH

INTERVIEWER: How old?

RUTH: Eighteen.

INTERVIEWER: And you are living at home now?

RUTH: Yes.

INTERVIEWER: What are you doing with your days, do you work?

RUTH: Go to school.

INTERVIEWER: Do you have a job also?

RUTH: Yes.

INTERVIEWER: What do you do?

RUTH: I work in a bookstore.

INTERVIEWER: And that is after school? You are still in high school?

RUTH: Yes.

INTERVIEWER: Do you have plans to go to college?

RUTH: Yeah.

INTERVIEWER: How did you feel about TOUGHLOVE in the beginning? You can say whatever you want.

RUTH: I hated it.

INTERVIEWER: Why?

RUTH: I just did.

INTERVIEWER: How was it affecting your life?

RUTH: It wasn't, in the beginning, at all.

INTERVIEWER: What did you think that it was? Did you have any idea what it was all about?

RUTH: Not really.

INTERVIEWER: Was there anything about TOUGHLOVE that was helpful to you?

RUTH: Yeah, I guess.

INTERVIEWER: How was it helpful?

RUTH: Got me off drugs.

INTERVIEWER: Did it hinder you in any way? Did it keep you from doing what you wanted?

RUTH: Not in the beginning.

INTERVIEWER: How about when your parents laid the law down? Gave you some rules to follow? Did you hate that?

RUTH: Yeah.

INTERVIEWER: How did TOUGHLOVE change your parents?

RUTH: They're stricter.

INTERVIEWER: Any other ways? Do they act differently?

RUTH: No.

INTERVIEWER: Did you get any surprises from TOUGH-LOVE?

RUTH: What do you mean?

INTERVIEWER: Did anything surprise you about what your parents were doing?

RUTH: Yeah.

INTERVIEWER: What surprised you?

RUTH: They were kicking me out of the house.

INTERVIEWER: Why was that a surprise?

RUTH: It just was.

INTERVIEWER: What was being kicked out of the house like?

RUTH: It wasn't good.

INTERVIEWER: Why not?

RUTH: It just wasn't.

INTERVIEWER: Where did you go when this happened?

RUTH: To a friend's house.

INTERVIEWER: How long did you stay there?

RUTH: A week.

INTERVIEWER: Did you like it?

RUTH: No.

INTERVIEWER: Why not?

RUTH: I didn't like the people I was staying with.

INTERVIEWER: Why not?

RUTH: My friend I didn't like anymore.

INTERVIEWER: How do you feel about TOUGHLOVE now?

RUTH: No way.

INTERVIEWER: Do you know any other kids that are involved, are any of your other friends' parents involved in TOUGHLOVE?

RUTH: Yes.

INTERVIEWER: How are they doing now?

RUTH: I don't know.

INTERVIEWER: Have you made any new friends from TOUGHLOVE?

RUTH: No.

INTERVIEWER: Did you have couseling during this period?

RUTH: Yes.

INTERVIEWER: And how was that, did you like that?

RUTH: I didn't like it.

INTERVIEWER: Why not?

RUTH: Because I just didn't like it.

INTERVIEWER: What was it about that you didn't like?

RUTH: I just didn't like it.

INTERVIEWER: That really says a lot, Ruth. Because people were asking questions about yourself?

RUTH: I guess.

INTERVIEW WITH A FRIEND OF RUTH'S—STACY

INTERVIEWER: Did you have something from the top of your head that you would like to say? What do you know about TOUGHLOVE?

STACY: Only what I heard and saw from Ruth. The first time she came back from it she was really shaken up from it. They were not nice to her, they were obnoxious to her. She didn't know what was going on, they didn't explain anything to her. She was totally confused. She had no idea what was going on. She could have been helped another way, I think. I didn't think she needed that. I don't think that that is what stopped her from doing the drugs. I think her parents did because they got stricter.

INTERVIEWER: How do you think that her parents got stricter? What do you think helped her parents?

STACY: I don't know. I guess the group meetings helped with that. Her parents set down the laws, she had to follow them or she couldn't live in the house. And she couldn't stand any of the people they were sending her to. She didn't have a choice. But that worked.

INTERVIEWER: Do you see a change in Ruth?

STACY: Oh yeah.

INTERVIEWER: How so?

STACY: She got off drugs, she got her act together. She started taking school more seriously.

INTERVIEWER: Do you see a change in her parents?

STACY: They are stricter. I guess if it started again, they would be even stricter. They know now that she's off drugs. They don't have to be so strict.

INTERVIEWER: What do you think about kids and school and drugs? Do you think society is different now?

STACY: Than when?

INTERVIEWER: Ten years ago.

STACY: Oh yeah, definitely.

INTERVIEWER: How so?

STACY: School is much harder to get through without getting involved in drugs. It's much more a part of school. You get pushed into it. When I tell my mother what goes on in school, she just can't believe that these things go on. People selling drugs so openly. It's pretty bad.

INTERVIEWER: So it's hard to go to school and not do drugs?

STACY: Yeah.

INTERVIEWER: Have you ever been to any of the parent support group meetings?

STACY: No.

INTERVIEWER: Do you know what they do there? Do you know what TOUGHLOVE is all about?

STACY: No. I just know that they gossip.

INTERVIEWER: What do you mean?

STACY: I know they talk about all our friends. They talked about us a lot. What we did that was wrong.

INTERVIEWER: Do you think they found out who was involved in drugs and who wasn't?

STACY: For the most part they had it pretty right.

INTERVIEWER: Do you know any other kids that have been involved in TOUGHLOVE?

STACY: Yes. A few of my other friends.

INTERVIEWER: How are they now? Do you notice a change in them?

STACY: One of them has changed, and the others, as far as I know, have not changed.

INTERVIEWER: What kind of changes do you see?

STACY: The one girl changed much like Ruth did. She straightened herself out. The other two girls are exactly as they were before. They haven't changed at all.

INTERVIEWER: Do you think that they have been involved with TOUGHLOVE the same amount of time?

STACY: They are not really actively involved.

INTERVIEWER: So you are saying that the parents have not continued in TOUGHLOVE so the kids haven't really changed?

STACY: Right.

The Harolds are parents who disliked taking those hard stands but their son Brad forced their hand each time. All of us have to learn at our own pace. It took a truly active community to help Brad.

In his alcohol addiction Brad saw TOUGHLOVE as being "against him." Later he came to understand that the community was against his addiction, not him.

The Harolds have been greatly influenced by Alcoholics Anonymous and sometimes use the language of A.A. You can feel their pain as they speak and you can sense that problems with kids don't magically end. Perhaps they need to make some new bottom lines to help them deal with their son.

INTERVIEWER: Why did you seek out TOUGHLOVE?
DAD: I think we were really desperate for help. We had kind of tried everything independent and it wasn't working, so we knew we needed some outside help. We started by going to the rehab program, they have like family counseling. It wasn't exactly family counseling, it was sort of a

parental guidance program that they had once a week.

INTERVIEWER: What was it that was going on in your household that brought you to... ?

DAD: Well, our son was totally out of control.

INTERVIEWER: What kinds of things was he doing?

DAD: You name it. Every weekend incidents of drunkenness, coming in late at all hours of the night. Doing nothing that we asked. Absolutely nothing. His life was in total turmoil. He was involved with the police, speeding, accidents with his car, problems at school or attending school, drunkenness. He would come home drunk. We needed help. Plus endless arguments, very violent arguments at home, pushing, shoving. We were getting to the point where we were getting real physical violence in the house. That is what we feared. We knew we had to do something.

INTERVIEWER: What kinds of things did you try before that, you said you tried some other things before TOUGHLOVE?

DAD: I guess we did the things that we thought would work and seemed to work for the other children, but after a while the things we were doing began to deteriorate to screaming and shouting and threats. We tried punishment or we tried disciplinary response to his bizarre behavior. But it wouldn't work, he just wouldn't do anything that we told him to do.

MOM: We did go to counseling.

INTERVIEWER: That was my next question.

MOM: That was early. We didn't really know that he had a problem. We really didn't know what was wrong with him. We just decided that we would go to counseling. We went to two different types of counseling, we went to Dell Clinic. We went there, we brought all of the kids with us, and after about eight times we decided that we were just throwing our money away because he was just sitting there and saying nothing. And then we did try this man, he just took us and Brad in his own home and he sort of made us feel that we were a little too tough on him. He suggested we give in a little bit. Try this and try that. It was just a big farce. Brad would say what he thought he should say.

INTERVIEWER: Was he a psychologist?

MOM: No, he was a family counselor. And nothing changed. Brad got worse.

DAD: He kept getting worse gradually. Brad kept saying that it wasn't any good and he didn't really support the counseling. And all the time, the counselor disguised the real problem, which was drug/alcohol related. Of course we really didn't see it then.

MOM: We really didn't know what the problem was. We really couldn't identify why he was acting the way he was. He occasionally had too much to drink, but we thought that maybe he was allergic to alcohol. I had all these excuses for him. He would always swear up and down that he had only two drinks and yet he could hardly see straight.

INTERVIEWER: How did that feel to you two at that point?

DAD: Total frustration. Not being able to influence your own child.

MOM: We were really so involved with him that our other children were suffering. We didn't think of anything but him. It was over a period of many years that this was going on.

INTERVIEWER: How long were you with TOUGHLOVE?

MOM: Since May of 1980. Brad already was not living at home at the time.

INTERVIEWER: What were the circumstances of his leaving home?

MOM: We had asked him to leave twice because of his intolerable behavior. At the time we came to TOUGHLOVE, he had been out of our home since February of that year and he insisted that he would not pay board. He was sort of using us. He should at least, since he was working full-time, give us a token.

INTERVIEWER: How old was he at this point?

MOM: He had just turned eighteen. He would come to our home and he would be in his car and go around the side of the house with his electrical plug and hook it up to a heater and put it in his car so that when we would wake up in the morning, he was living in the driveway in his car. He would glare at us.

DAD: We really didn't know what to do for a while. We felt kind of guilty having our son leave. In fact the night that we had him leave in February, he came home very drunk and nasty. It was two in the morning Sunday when I had him leave the house. We really felt at that point that we had to take some risks in this.

Tragic as they may be we felt that we had to start taking risks and turn this thing around. That very night that I threw him out, he left the house slamming and banging doors, got into his car, drove down the block and drove up someone's driveway and across the lawn, and did a very sharp turn and side-skidded across our lawn and down over the curb like a madman. Starsky and Hutch scene. But that was the kind of bizarre behavior that would come from these incidents. He would punch things, put holes in doors, throw things. Just very disruptive, fighting with his brothers.

MOM: Whatever he needed he would just take, he would never ask.

DAD: He was stealing outside the home, he did some breaking into homes.

MOM: He was involved with a young fellow that would break into garages, they would take things and sell them. He took a pair of skis. He came home with them and in fact we didn't know until a year after that he sold a pair of skis.... He was involved with another pair of skis and the police, who knew him from other incidents, called up and asked if he would testify against this kid because the kid was blaming my son for the whole thing. Brad did go to court and testify against him.

INTERVIEWER: Are you still involved with TOUGHLOVE?

MOM: We're still involved. We don't go as regularly as we used to.

INTERVIEWER: Why do you stay with it?

MOM: We've gotten so much help from it and everything seems to be fine now.

DAD: Occasionally we have some problems. It's really a good place to go and discuss your problems with those who have similar problems. Others make suggestions that you sometimes may not think of. We do appreciate the active suggestions that you get from TOUGHLOVE. We went to Al-Anon for a while but I flet uncomfortable there. It was mostly women. I was the only male. Also Al-Anon seemed to be less inclined to volunteer ideas on how you might solve your problems. It seemed to be more of a setup where people would just come and talk about their problems and very few would have any comments. Solutions did not seem to come or were not offered. Now we can help others.

INTERVIEWER: When you went to TOUGHLOVE, what was the hardest thing for you to accept?

DAD: I think the concept of letting go, which is letting your child be responsible for the consequences of his actions. As parents, we think we have to solve all their problems or anticipate the consequences of their actions. It's the same as preaching. Our kid was stealing from vegetable gardens, whatever he could get his hands on in the summertime. He had been coming by our house. We knew that he had entered the house a number of times when it was locked and had taken food. It was difficult to come to the next step, which was to have him arrested and press charges. That's where TOUGHLOVE helped.

INTERVIEWER: What were the charges?

MOM: Breaking and entering our home. To see him come into court with handcuffs on was the worst thing. To know that he was in a horrible place.

INTERVIEWER: Prison?

MOM: Yes, he was in there for ten days and I didn't bail him out. That was hard.

DAD: We got frantic phone calls.

MOM: He kept calling and we wouldn't accept his phone call. I did go once to the prison and I guess I shouldn't have gone. It was hard. He really wanted me to bail him out and I didn't see him again until he was in court.

INTERVIEWER: Were you involved with any other parents in your group? Did you have anyone going along with you?

MOM: Two other women went with us. In fact when I went to visit him in prison, another woman went with me.

DAD: We kind of bargained with the court-appointed defense counselor. The defense counselor talked to us and we expressed our real concerns—that he was an alcoholic, he needed professional help, and that's all we were trying to work toward. At that point the attorney, his counsel, arranged to get him off the hook. To have the charges dropped providing Brad would agree to go to some kind of counseling. Brad agreed, he said he would go to A.A. meetings or whatever.

MOM: He promised that he would attend meetings. . . .

DAD: He promised that he would stop drinking. . . .

MOM: He promised that he would attend meetings if I would drop charges. If I didn't drop the charges, he would have to go back to prison and have to wait until his case came up again, which was like in two more months. We didn't want to go through with that so we dropped the charges.

DAD: That turned out to be a mistake on our part because he didn't follow through.

MOM: No he didn't, he just walked out. We just said good-bye to him at the door and that was the end of that.

DAD: We didn't see him again until he was arrested a second time.

INTERVIEWER: And what happened then?

DAD: Since he had left high school, he had four jobs. It's amazing, I guess, that he held a job for any length of time, but he would manage to hold a job for a few weeks to get some money together to maintain some minimal survival. And this went on from the time he graduated from high school in 1979 and here we are in the summer of '80 and for a whole year he had survived. He would get fired and find another one somehow and get fired again. After he had been arrested the first time, and then proceeded to do nothing, he did go look for a job, he didn't have a job at the time. He went to a warehouse to try and get a job and hooked up with someone in the warehouse who drank also.

MOM: The man was sitting there and said to Brad, Why don't we chip in and get a case of beer? So Brad went in on a case of beer with this guy. Within a couple of hours he had finished more than half a case of beer. He was drifting. He really had no place to live or sleep.

DAD: He decided that he would sleep on the railroad in a boxcar. He was in the process of breaking into the boxcar looking for one that had room for a body and was then arrested by the police. This was his second arrest and they took him to the county prison. That night we got a call from the detective who arrested him, who was really concerned about him. Brad seemed to be deeply depressed, suicidal. The detective almost regretted that he had arrested him. He was really concerned about his mental state. Of course we were too. We thought that maybe the crisis was coming. I then called a psychologist up in the county prison and talked to him some. They were interviewing him. He was beginning to accept the seriousness of the problem that he was having with alcohol. We also began to hear that he was interested in coming back and living with us in peace. The time seemed right then and he was begging to be bailed out of prison. We left him there a couple of days. Then we decided that the time seemed right, we were getting reports from the psychologist in the prison that he really wanted to turn himself around, that he had suffered enough. We went to the magistrate's office. Brought two friends from TOUGHLOVE, two male friends. When the jailer brought him where you paid the bail, Brad thought he was going home, but he really wasn't.

We weren't going to accept him into our home. The two friends took him to their house and he stayed there for a while. We just wanted to keep the surprises coming so he wouldn't get set and start scheming. They really become brilliant schemers and con artists. The very next night we had him come to our home, with these two male friends. We had a negotiation. In the meantime, one of the male friends that afternoon took him to the rehab and set up an interview with some of the counselors there. Apparently at that rehab interview, he began to identify himself as alcoholic. Of course on numerous occasions before I had told him that he may be an alcoholic and of course he wouldn't listen. I told him of blood relatives who were alcoholics. He wouldn't listen to that at all. I think at the time his response was he didn't drink hard liquor anyway. He had switched from hard liquor to beer. So beer was O.K.

MOM: We were nervous about him coming home even into our home after all that was done, we still had a lot of distrust. We went though a lot and we were not really satisfied with him just coming home and promising to go to meetings. We felt that we needed more than that. We did have this negotiation. Then our TOUGHLOVE suport person just kept popping up for the next couple of days, taking Brad off, talking to him, went shopping with him. . . .

INTERVIEWER: This is another member of TOUGHLOVE?

DAD: Another member of TOUGHLOVE. Even

at this point Brad felt that he could solve his problems through willpower and by attending A.A. meetings. He still had not accepted what we wanted was to put him into a rehabilitation center. He didn't feel that he needed rehabilitation. He really seemed sincere at this point but he seemed to have this pressing, almost overpowering drive to go get a job quick and make some money and pay off all his fines. At this point he had hundreds of dollars of fines against him. He had been stopped so many times for auto violations. It was an endless series. . . . His solution had been to get a job, make money. It was kind of a struggle over the next few days to convince him to go to a rehab.

MOM: We had a lot of people working in our behalf. Youth Services, TOUGHLOVE, police . . .

DAD: But he still was really there.

MOM: We had an appointment Sunday morning.

DAD: He was gradually accepting the concept of rehab very slowly, very reluctantly. Even Sunday morning as they were getting ready to leave and having breakfast, there were times he would talk for ten minutes at length on how he could do it himself, he didn't need rehab. Then he would accept rehab. He'll be O.K. he'll make it. It was a struggle. During one of those interludes, we had all his stuff ready to go, during a ten-minute stretch where he was again accepting the concept of rehab, we just took him out to the car and away we went. About halfway there the car broke down. Do you believe that? Later on he told us that he was tempted to run away at that point. He was motioning, he was walking along the road. He was very much tempted to at that point leave. We called ahead and we knew that eighty-five percent of the population were in his age bracket. We felt strongly that once we got him up here he would eventually accept it. When we got up there, as soon as we walked into the door and looked around, you could see the acceptance on his face. The tension seemed to abate. He liked the looks of the place.

MOM: We felt that because it was far away, it would be the best place for him. Living away it would be hard for him to get home. He really is an outdoorsman, we thought the surroundings would be good for him.

DAD: A lot of deer there. It was right in the middle of the woods.

MOM: He stayed about six weeks.

DAD: He reentered later for sort of a refresher for one week.

INTERVIEWER: Did he complete treatment at A.A.?

MOM: Yes he did.

INTERVIEWER: He came back to live at your house?

MOM: Yes.

DAD: Before he came to the house we had talked with the counselor to see if they thought he should come back to the house. We had no reservations about taking him back but at this point we wanted to have the best chances to succeed and we would have done whatever they recommended. They did recommend that we bring him home, they thought it would work. They felt very strongly that he really wanted to return home. He thought that he had to make amends for the past.

MOM: We were nervous that he would get calls from old friends, and how would he be able to handle that? Would I be able to handle it? That type of thing.

DAD: We were warned not to be too surprised if there were some slips. We were really afraid that he would slip, and how would we react?

INTERVIEWER: Did you bring this to your parents group at all? While you were involved, did you ever talk about these kinds of fears?

MOM: Oh I think so. We would express how we felt every time we would visit him. How we were worried about him coming home and how we were going to handle it. We were very open with everybody because we were, I guess, the second family in our group whose child had been in rehab and it was more or less new for everybody.

DAD: I recall that it was recommended that we put our faith in the counselor's ways of determining. They look for the signs, should the kid return home or not, should he go to a halfway house. They all felt that he should return home. We did have faith in their judgment.

INTERVIEWER: When you first got involved with TOUGH-LOVE, what did you hope to get from it?

DAD: Peace in the family, more than anything. The family was in total chaos. We didn't know where to turn. What else to do. We thought that we had tried so many things and they didn't work. You're so frustrated, you're so powerless that your imagination becomes frozen. You can't really cope.

INTERVIEWER: It's like beating your head against the wall, over and over?

DAD: Yeah, beating your head against the wall. You are so emotionally involved, it's really difficult to come up with fresh ideas and really to look objectively at what you are doing and be able to critique yourself and say, Gee, maybe we're doing this wrong, maybe we should try that. Whereas other parents, although they are having trouble in their own home, can listen to your problems more objectively and, not being so emotionally involved, see things that you can't see. And vice versa.

MOM: If it is you that is wrong, you might be able to accept it from another parent rather than your own child. . . .

DAD: Or your own spouse, because we would fight and argue. We were so frustrated that we would have continual battles.

MOM: Blame each other. Blame everything.

INTERVIEWER: Did you get the peace?

DAD: When he left, there was a tremendous burden lifted off our shoulders when he left the house. Even when he was still very sick and very active as an alcoholic, we had suffered, the family as a whole, so much that it was a relief to have him leave. It was so sad to realize that he was destroying himself out there. But it almost got to the point of where what had to be done was for the survival of the family. The family, even knowing that he was out there suffering and leading an agonizing life, we weren't confronted with it daily. You weren't fighting daily. There wasn't the constant turmoil. The phone calls at all hours of the night, the police, other drug users, or whatever. We used to get endless phone calls where there would be a hang-up if the right voice wouldn't answer. There was peace in a sense that the real right-now problems disappeared. Of course that problem kept looming up all the time. What can we do to help him?

MOM: We did feel that we could call other people and talk to them. We weren't the only ones going through this.

DAD: I think that unless people actually go through this they cannot understand the agony and the hurt. We found that unless the person suffered as we did, they couldn't understand a child leaving home. They just couldn't identify with that. It's almost like forsaking your own flesh and blood.

INTERVIEWER: What rewards did you get from the whole experience while involved with TOUGH-LOVE?

DAD: Rewards? The ultimate reward is that he's straight, we feel that TOUGHLOVE contributed very much to that kind of peace of mind. As much peace of mind that we could get during the period when he was out of the house. The rewards of seeing it work because you were told that you had to have a crisis. It's very hard to accept this concept of crisis. Because it seems like almost a risk. The crisis may mean that he could commit suicide, he may kill himself or someone else. A horrible accident. These were all possibilities too, that could have been part of the crisis. But the reward for us was the crisis came and it brought about good results for him and for us. He's been straight now since Labor Day 1980. That is a blessing. A.A. took over once he got straightened out. The crisis came about much sooner because of our association with TOUGHLOVE.

INTERVIEWER: Can you think of any other risks that you took?

MOM: Well, the risk of sending him up to rehab and hoping that he would stay there and not run away, and this was his last chance. We told him that this was a gift we were giving him, we couldn't go through any more of what we had been through.

INTERVIEWER: How about after the rehab? Were there risks after that?

MOM: There is a risk because they are back into society again.

DAD: The very first weekend he was home he wanted to see some friends in the back, he was offered some hash by one of the neighbor boys that quick. The same boy, before he went into rehab, when Brad was talking to his friends about him maybe going into rehab, this very same boy was reminding him that if he goes to rehab that means that you can never drink again, do you really want to go through with this, you would never be able to do drugs again. That was a risk too. We were so afraid that he would fall back in his old habits.

INTERVIEWER: Was it all worth it?

MOM: Oh yeah. It was worth it. He still has problems.

DAD: He still has a lot of maturing to do. We had heard before that their emotional development is suspended during the time you're doing. Of course he had been doing and using for a number of years. We can now see that it is true. He's kind of reliving his early teenage years. He's kind of immature at this point. He still seems reluctant to accept responsibility. Where before we used to have arguments over his drinking we now have arguments over his reluctance to accept simple responsibility.

INTERVIEWER: What were your relatives' reactions to TOUGHLOVE? How did the other kids feel about it?

DAD: We were really more involved with the TOUGHLOVE members than any family member.

INTERVIEWER: How did your other kids feel about it?

MOM: Well, they thought we were right as far as we had put up with so much that it was ... they were really relieved.

DAD: They supported us.

MOM: They were not totally supportive of him going to prison, they really didn't understand that.

INTERVIEWER: Did they try to interfere at any point with what you were doing?

DAD: No. My reaction was that the seventeen-year-old reacted kind of funny to it.

MOM: Well, he was so close in age to his brother and I guess that he was identifying too with him. He would occasionally have a

drink and he would think, Are they going
to do the same thing to me? It was hard
for him to understand that.

INTERVIEWER: How did you handle his reaction?

MOM: We just told him that this was good for
Brad and he left it at that.

INTERVIEWER: As far as the community aspect, do you
feel through your experience you've gotten
to know and understand social services.
Did you have much contact with them?

MOM: With Youth Services we did. Since this
agency lost its funds, it is no longer in
existence.

INTERVIEWER: Do you think that through TOUGHLOVE
you understand the agency network better?
Do you know there are places to go?

MOM: Oh yeah.

INTERVIEWER: How about the police? And the schools?
Do you feel you understand them better?

MOM: I think so. I do think you can get things
accomplished if you are not blaming all
these different people. You go to them
and talk to them.

INTERVIEWER: How about the police, what was their
reaction to your parents group here?

MOM: The police were very supportive of us,
helping us to do whatever we had to do.

DAD: I really didn't have that much contact
with them.

INTERVIEWER: Did any of the police come to your group?
Did they ever want to know more about
TOUGHLOVE?

DAD: There were a couple of detectives who
came.

MOM: We had some parole officers.

INTERVIEWER: Were they cooperative?

MOM: We had a couple of district judges come

to our meetings, they were very cooperative. They sent other parents to our groups. We had the schools. They know what TOUGHLOVE is about. There were some parents who said that their children would be responsible for their own actions and that they were not going to go up to the school every time their child got into some kind of trouble.

DAD: I think the schools think that of course parents are responsible for their children; that's true, there is no question about that. But they also feel that by informing the parents of what's happening with their child, they expect the parents to somehow have a positive impact on this kid and the kid's behavior will somehow improve. I don't see how that could ever come to pass because when you are in a situation where the kid is addicted to drugs or alcohol and pretty much into serious trouble, the parents find themselves powerless. They can't help or support the school, because they can't get the kid to do anything in their own home, let alone in the school. In these bizarre cases, I somehow think the schools and parents have to somehow work closer together to precipitate crises. Our crisis had come about after Brad had left school.

MOM: I think some of the parents that are coming to the meetings are having the schools cooperate.

DAD: We really did not get on him until he graduated from high school and that may have been a mistake. While he was in his senior year, we knew we had a serious problem and we were bewildered as to what to do. But I think in the back of our heads was a no-no to have him get all messed up in school. We kind of felt that once he graduated, once he got a job, things would straighten out. Well, that was not really smart thinking, it was false thinking. False hopes. Wishful thinking.

MOM: We thought that it would all go away.

DAD: We should have precipitated the crisis right then and there when he was still in school. We didn't do that. I guess that everyone thinks the same thing. No, we can't do it now, he's in school. The really most important thing is to get the head straight and if that means missing school for a whole year, it's worth it.

INTERVIEWER: Do you feel that there are more supportive people around you now?

MOM: I think so, more people understand about it. It's been given a lot of public exposure. Radio and television.

INTERVIEWER: Do you personally feel that you have more support out there now? If something were to happen again, would you have the support that you need?

MOM: I think so.

DAD: The people I have talked to and who have heard about TOUGHLOVE, I get good feedback from them. It seems they are interested in the program. It's got a lot of hope.

INTERVIEWER: Have you made any friends from the program?

MOM: Oh yeah. Very good friends.

INTERVIEWER: Would you recommend TOUGHLOVE?

MOM: Oh yeah. We do tell people about it.

INTERVIEW WITH SON BRAD

INTERVIEWER: How did you feel about TOUGHLOVE in the beginning?

BRAD: I didn't really understand it so I thought it was just threatening to me.

INTERVIEWER: How so?

BRAD: I just thought it threatened kids. It was just against kids. Parents were joining forces against us. It was very threatening to me.

INTERVIEWER: It was going to keep you from doing what you wanted?

BRAD: Yeah.

INTERVIEWER: Did you find out that it was helpful to you at all at any point?

BRAD: The last time I was in jail, when I got out, one of the parents that they knew from TOUGHLOVE took me around a lot and that really helped. I needed somebody to help me out just at that time.

INTERVIEWER: Did it hinder you at all?

BRAD: It kind of hindered communications with my parents when I wanted to get my way. They wouldn't talk to me, they would talk to me through other members of TOUGHLOVE. Made things very difficult for me. Getting my stuff out of the house or getting certain things that I needed.

INTERVIEWER: So it kept you from what you wanted to get?

BRAD: Yeah.

INTERVIEWER: How do you think it changed your parents?

BRAD: They got to see that they were not the

only ones with these problems and they had support of people helping them.

INTERVIEWER: Did they seem different to you?

BRAD: They were more calm in situations and more sure of what to do. Before they were hyper. Before they were really emotional about dealing with situations, and since they went to TOUGHLOVE they now knew what they were going to do and they did it and that's it. No fuss.

INTERVIEWER: Did you get any surprises from TOUGH-LOVE?

BRAD: Yeah, I came to my house to get something to eat one day, after I was thrown out, and I got charges brought against me, so that really surprised me.

INTERVIEWER: And what happened?

BRAD: I was in jail for two weeks. My parents charged me with criminal trespassing.

INTERVIEWER: That was a big surprise. You were in jail for a while, that was the first time that that had happened and then it happened again. How are you doing now?

BRAD: Real good. I'm having a great time.

INTERVIEWER: What are you doing with yourself these days?

BRAD: I'm going to school for drafting.

INTERVIEWER: Are you doing that full-time? Going to school?

BRAD: Yeah, eight to three.

INTERVIEWER: Do you work at all now?

BRAD: I'm getting ready to look for a part-time job. I go to meetings in the evenings.

INTERVIEWER: What kind of meetings?

BRAD: Narcotics Anonymous.

INTERVIEWER: You said that you are staying with people now that don't drink or take drugs.

BRAD: I mostly hang around recovering addicts.

INTERVIEWER: What's it like now for you out in the streets?

BRAD: I feel more confident with myself.

INTERVIEWER: You went into a rehab, right?

BRAD: Yeah.

INTERVIEWER: And how long did you stay there?

BRAD: About a month and a half.

INTERVIEWER: How did you feel about the place?

BRAD: I had heard all kinds of crazy stories about it and I really didn't know what to expect. Once I got there I found out that there was a lot of people like me that had the same problems that I had, that I thought only I had. Then I knew that I was at the right place.

INTERVIEWER: Is it hard to find friends now?

BRAD: Not really. I have more friends now than I ever had. Real friends.

INTERVIEWER: How do you feel about TOUGHLOVE now?

BRAD: I don't really know a lot about it. I know it serves a purpose.

INTERVIEWER: Which was, what do you think that was?

BRAD: Place of refuge for parents in distress. Learn how to cope.

INTERVIEWER: I asked how you felt.

BRAD: The only thing that it did for me was to get a better relationship with my parents. We deal with our problems now head on instead of letting them build up. Just take care of things as they come up. Instead of letting all kinds of frustrations build up. Get into fights.

This interview reads like the nightmare many parents have lived through. The Brooks's story is a classic tale of the havoc wrought by drug-abusing kids and the difficult steps needed to turn the process of abuse around. Over and over Janice Brooks emphasizes the importance of giving and getting support.

INTERVIEWER: You are Mrs. Brooks, and how many children do you have?

MOM: Three.

INTERVIEWER: What are their ages?

MOM: Bruce is twenty-one, Ted is nineteen, and Chris is sixteen.

INTERVIEWER: Why did you seek out TOUGHLOVE?

MOM: It happened a year ago. We were at wits' end with our oldest son.

INTERVIEWER: What was going on?

MOM: He was totally out of control. He was going to school at the time, but he wasn't really into it.

INTERVIEWER: Was he skipping school?

MOM: Yes. He was going to Devon State for only three days a week.

INTERVIEWER: He was at college?

MOM: Yes. We wanted him to get a part-time job. He just would not. We did not know where he was.

INTERVIEWER: Was he commuting to Devon State or was he going to a local campus?

MOM: He was commuting to a local campus. He had a lot of time on his hands. But was not making use of it and was not doing well in school. Before, in high school, he was an excellent student.

INTERVIEWER: You are talking about the changes in his behavior?

MOM: Yes. In the summer before he started college, he had a construction job and he had to commute all the way to New York. He had to leave here by six in the morning. He was staying out till three, four o'clock, getting two, three hours of sleep and I couldn't understand how could a kid who always required a lot of sleep manage on this. We were at wits' end, we didn't know what to do with him. We tried to talk to him. My husband was losing sleep and time at work because he couldn't function properly. I was worried about him. Basically what was going on was that everything seemed to be falling apart and we were trying to keep it a secret from everybody. Not talking about it to anybody. I had a hard time explaining at work why I was upset all the time. Finally we were very concerned, we confronted him, asking him if he had a drug problem. Of course, he denied it. He said, I'm just a little mixed up with my life right now. I have to have time to

think things out and get my head together.
Finally in January of last year, we got a
call from the police. Testimony from a
burglar from our neighborhood showed
that our two boys were hooked on speed
by a drug pusher. So that comes down to
what we were concerned about. The
nineteen-year-old son was not as deeply
involved as was Bruce. After the police
called and told us this, I said, My God,
we don't know that much about drugs.
They told us they would get a drug
package together and if we would stop
by they would give it to us. When I got
there to pick it up, an officer wanted to
speak to me and he introduced me to
TOUGHLOVE. He was the crime prevention officer. He said Lee Scribner was
beginning a chapter and gave me Lee's
number and he asked would I be interested. And I said definitely. He asked
me if I had known about it and I said
that I had read about it in the newspaper
about six months before and I thought
that I could never do what they said.
About putting a kid out of the house, I
couldn't handle that. But when it got to
this point, six months later, our problems
were much worse. I was ready for it
then.

INTERVIEWER: Had you sought help previously?

MOM: No. The only thing that I did, a month
before the officer called us, was speak to
my family doctor and I asked him what
could I do and he told me try to communicate with him. He asked me when the
communication broke down and I said

when he became a teenager. It just got worse and worse. I was surprised that he didn't recommend a psychologist. I really had no experience with therapy before and I didn't know where to turn. I was also trying to hide it. I didn't want anyone to know. We are trying to solve these problems.

INTERVIEWER: What were you feeling when all of this was going on?

MOM: I felt embarrassment. Where did I go wrong? Felt guilt. Blaming my husband— our marriage almost broke up. Blaming myself. I was just blaming everything, blaming the schools. It was a nightmare.

INTERVIEWER: How long have you been with TOUGH-LOVE?

MOM: I started in the Lakeside Chapter a year ago next week. I was there the first night.

INTERVIEWER: Why did you stay?

MOM: Because I found so much help and support. Really got control of my house again. The support, I just can't say enough about that. Like I said, I was hiding it. I didn't have anyone to talk to. When we went there everybody was so supportive. They knew what I was going through. There were some who were there who had already gone through what we were going through, that were helpful. I didn't feel alone anymore, which I had felt before. We're pretty much through our crisis. I am helping others and giving support to them, because I feel that I have taken a lot from the program and I want to give back.

INTERVIEWER: What was the hardest thing for you to accept about TOUGHLOVE?

MOM: I guess saying to your kid, If you don't shape up, you've got to ship out.

INTERVIEWER: Did you have to do that?

MOM: Yes. He wouldn't cooperate with the rules that we had set down.

INTERVIEWER: What kinds of things was he doing?

MOM: Staying out late. He eventually dropped out of college about a month before I came to TOUGHLOVE. Then he wasn't doing anything, no job, just lying around. No money. I couldn't understand how he could put gas in his car. He was still driving his car.

INTERVIEWER: Was he on drugs at that point?

MOM: Yes. I guess it was at our second meeting at TOUGHLOVE where I found all the sharing. Judge Quinn came to our meeting. I saw him watching me while I was talking, he knew something. He told us that night, if there was any way that he could help us to please call and he was willing to help. I did have occasion to call him because my son was out of the house and his car was in our name and he had had three drinking fines. He was still drinking and I was afraid to let him have the car, that he was going to hurt himself, hurt someone else. We told him when he left that he could not have the car. He was giving us a hard time about that because he did pay for the car himself. I had a legal question in that regard. I called him and asked him about it. He said, Keep the car, it's yours, it's in your name, and don't let him have it. If you will come to my office, I will tell you about your son. He told us that he was dealing, he knew it, and he was under surveillance.

INTERVIEWER: How did that feel?

MOM: It hurt. It hurt a lot.

INTERVIEWER: Were you surprised?

MOM: Shocked. I couldn't ever believe that my son would ever do a thing like that.

INTERVIEWER: How did your husband feel?

MOM: Pretty much the same. You have high hopes for your children. They were always good kids. Never really gave us big problems. He was always a good kid in school. The teachers always gave me good reports. I couldn't believe that a kid like that could turn into such a monster.

INTERVIEWER: So you had given him a chance to leave and he decided to leave?

MOM: Our first step was the contract. To try to get rules set down, so he would know exactly what we expected. We really didn't have our rules clear and concise. "Play it by ear" kind of thing. We could always trust him. We could trust him to accept responsibility. We had the contract all set up and he was to be here at seven-thirty. He called about a half hour before saying he was on a job interview, and I knew that he was lying. I told him that if he was not home by seven, he could drop the car in the driveway and not come into the house. He didn't show up. It was his choice. It was very simple.

INTERVIEWER: What happened with the car?

MOM: He kept the car. The car did not come

back. Couple of days later, he came for his clothes, but he parked the car somewhere else. He walked. He and another boy came. By this time we had really had it. My husband came flying down the stairs saying, I don't want to see you, I want you out of this house. You cannot have your clothes. He was really upset. He took off down the street. My husband was in a rage. Later Bruce said, Dad, I never saw you so angry. I think my husband yelled after him that if he didn't return the car he would have a warrant for his arrest. For stealing the car. We could have done that but we didn't. We didn't have the heart to follow through on that. One night about a week later we came home from a TOUGHLOVE meeting and found a note in the door from the police. Apparently what had happened, he and another boy were sitting in the car in this neighborhood. The policeman came up behind them and he thought that the policeman was coming to arrest him and they panicked. They took off in the car, ran off from the police. At one point, they hopped out of the car, it was like a chase for a short distance, when they got to this certain spot, they both jumped out of the car and ran on foot. The policeman never found them but they had the car. They impounded it, they searched it, and they didn't find drugs, but they did find needles. They found a scale in the trunk. Apparently, he had been living out of the trunk. Some of his clothes were in there. All the policeman wanted to know was why were they sitting there. In the state of mind that he was in with the drugs, he didn't think straight. It just proved to him that he was out of control. After that we got the car back. I think it was only another three days later that he was picked up by the police. For harassment. He was walking at four A,M. in the morning alone in the neighborhood. He saw this fellow get out of another guy's car and walk up to his house. He asked to buy or to sell him something. The guy went in and called the police. Then the police picked up Bruce about a block away. From there Judge Quinn was trying to help us. Kind of a scare tactic. Kind of give him what a taste of prison was like. So they did take him up there but they didn't hold him because they didn't have enough on him. The following day we handed over drugs and paraphernalia that we had found in the house and we did have him arrested. He spent two days up at county prison. And from there he went to the New Life Program. He said, I could have friends bail me out but I'm not going to because I need help and I know I need help. Please get me out of here. That was tough.

INTERVIEWER: How did you decide about New Life?

MOM: I had heard a lot about it through some people from TOUGHLOVE. They recommended it highly. Lee Scribner and Shirley Borman. So that is how we decided on New Life.

INTERVIEWER: How did you handle getting him from prison to the rehab?

MOM: We had to go to Judge Quinn's office and have a hearing. The constable brought him from prison down to Judge Quinn's office and we met him there. That was a horrendous experience. He didn't have any cuffs on. It was tough having to see him looking the way he did. He was in a terrible state. I guess he had gone through withdrawal. In fact he didn't know how long he had been there.

INTERVIEWER: How long had he been out on the street?

MOM: He was out for one week when we asked him to go to a psychologist and he refused to go. In order for you to live here you must get some kind of help, we told him, and he refused that. He was out for one week and he called us at the end of that week and said that he would get help. Then he went to the psychologist. He went and the psychologist told him that he was a drug addict and that he needed in-patient care. We took him to New Life. He knew that he really needed help. Sylvia interviewed him. She came out and said that he should try the out-patient program and we were so angry at her. She didn't say he could handle it but she said, I think that we should let him try it. He had not had any other counseling. The New Life out-patient program has since closed down. He had an interview and they closed down before his interview came up so he was back home for a week waiting for this. The day he did not show up for his contract, he was also supposed to have counseling that day, he didn't show up for that. He was out on the street again. He was out on the street actually for two weeks. It was horrible. He hated us. We drove him to the New Life Program. He kept asking for something to eat and we were afraid that he would run and we would not stop. We just kept going. So when we got there he was playing on our sympathy. He told us later that he was faking and that he would have run.

I just want to add something that happened last week. My nineteen-year-old son, Ted, is still struggling and he's not completely off drugs. I'm scared that he is going to pull himself down again. What had happened at our meeting last week, my bottom line was to take him out to lunch and spend some time with him. We both needed that. It's very important, just the two of us. The following morning, before I had a chance to mention the lunch date, my husband had found pot in his car. We were very upset by it. What was really neat was that we had had the contract, anything to do with the car in that respect he loses his driving privileges for a week. So it was very simple: Well, Ted, here it is, we found this and you lose your driving privileges this week. He took his punishment. Normally, he would have ran out of the house. Lord knows what else. He even agreed to go to lunch with me. It shows that we have a lot more control. He's come a long way.

INTERVIEWER: When you first went to TOUGHLOVE what did you hope to get?

MOM: I really didn't know what to expect. I hoped to get help. Find some solutions to our problems.

INTERVIEWER: And what did you get?

MOM: I got some solutions. I gained a lot of strength. I was very, very weak. One of these parents who were afraid to punish too heavy because your kid might hate you. That kind of thing. That was the tough part. I hurt for a long time. When we had our first counseling session, I was so nervous, it was ten days later and I was really dreading that. When he came in and in a happy mood, I couldn't believe it. I was amazed. I really thought that he was done with us and that I had lost him. But when he came in, how can I describe it? He looked happy.

INTERVIEWER: Was this a family session?

MOM: Yes. It was so nice. He was so happy to see us. He told me that he was happy that we put him there.

INTERVIEWER: Who was in on the session?

MOM: The whole family. I don't think that Ted went to the first one because he was having problems himself. It was just my husband, myself, and my sixteen-year-old son. We had a problem with Ted, we couldn't get him to go. He was having problems himself with drugs. It was kind of tough with him.

INTERVIEWER: What happened to him?

MOM: After we got Bruce situated, we started working on him. He was in twelfth grade at the time.

INTERVIEWER: He was the next youngest?

MOM: Yes. He was having problems in school for the past couple of years. His grades were just gradually declining. He was involved in sports and good at it. Good in football, et cetera. He had just been dropping all of that. By tenth grade he didn't do anything.

INTERVIEWER: So that was a big change?

MOM: Yes. He was also to the point where we would ground him and he would run right out of the house. We had no control there either. He was keeping his curfew. He abided by most of the rules but if there was a grounding, forget it, he would just run out.

INTERVIEWER: Had you sought help from anyone else aside from the psychologist?

MOM: This was after our second TOUGHLOVE meeting I believe. We didn't seek help from any other area. I was not familiar with psychology. I just didn't know where to turn. Then TOUGHLOVE came up and I started there. The reason we took him to that psychologist was for the drug evaluation.

INTERVIEWER: What was the outcome?

MOM: The outcome was that Bruce was diagnosed as a drug addict and needed in-patient care. Ted, he said, he was not sure exactly. He agreed with TOUGHLOVE and said to work with him.

INTERVIEWER: So he was supportive of TOUGHLOVE?

MOM: Yes he was, and in fact he came to some

of our meetings to get some more knowledge. He wasn't sure where Ted stood. Ted wasn't being honest with him. We tried for the contract and he refused. He left the house. He was going over every morning to a kid's house before school. I just didn't like what I thought was going on. I thought that they were going to get high, maybe he uses drugs there, maybe he picks them up there. It was so important to him that one day when I was going to drive him to school, because it was snowing and he wouldn't wear boots, so I said, I'm driving you, I don't want your feet all wet. We're backing out of the driveway and I said I would not go to Scott's house: I'm driving you to school, that's it. He jumped out of the car. Ran over to his friend's house. We were really sure then that something was going on. One of our bottom lines was to go to the principal. See if they would search him. We couldn't find anything here at all. So they did. The principal did search him, two friends, and found drugs on all of them. They all had to go to court. We were behind getting Ted into a rehab. We wanted that for him. He started outpatient counseling in the meantime before his hearing came up. I was even suspicious of him being high at one of his sessions. The other two boys went to court, got off with probation. When Ted went in, his probation officer told him that he would have to go to a rehab for two months. Ted went out that night and I don't know if he purposely did it, he did overdose. He was threatening suicide. Well, some kids had come to the door and said, Mrs. Brooks, come quick, Ted is freaking out. I went up to the field where he was and he was like a maniac. He was screaming. When he saw it was me he was just like an animal. It was awful. What it was was that he had taken Quaaludes with PCP and earlier in the day he had drunk a whole quart of whiskey. It had just completely freaked him out. I couldn't get him in the car. He was very strong. His legs were like rubber. He would try to run and he would fall down. But when his friends were trying to hold him down, he became very violent. They called the ambulance. The police came. The ambulance attendants couldn't get him into the ambulance. He would try running. They finally had to cuff him and put him in restraints. This was like nine Friday night. He didn't stop screaming or carrying on in the emergency room until six hours later. I found out that they had given him something to calm him down. It was a horrendous night. He was very angry at us. We were trying so hard to get him help and he didn't want it. Prior to that, before his hearing came up he was out of the house for six weeks living with a kid that he had met in school who wasn't even a friend. The reason he had left was because he would not go along with the contract. Finally after the six weeks the kid's mother started putting pressure on him, saying, Why are you not going home? She didn't understand what was going on. He did tell her the truth and I guess she thought we were a bit harsh. So one night she called me.

INTERVIEWER: What rewards do you feel that you got from TOUGHLOVE?

MOM: I'm feeling a lot better about myself. That I have control of my house again. I felt very weak before, now I feel much stronger. I feel good because I'm helping others. I've always been that type of person, I always like to help others. I have a problem reaching out for help. I feel like I can handle it myself. The rewards are just to have this family back together again. There are so many. We had the best Christmas this year that we have had in ages. It all started. The rehab was good. It all goes back to TOUGHLOVE. We got the help that both boys needed. Getting the family back together. Getting them back to their old self. I feel like I'm in control again.

INTERVIEWER: What risks have you taken?

MOM: Losing both boys. That was a risk. I was afraid that I would lose their love. I wondered if they would ever forgive us for that. But they did.

INTERVIEWER: Was it worth it?

MOM: It sure was.

INTERVIEWER: What kind of support did you get?

MOM: The phone calls and visits. It started when Bruce was out of the house. I was afraid because I knew that he had nowhere to go. I was afraid that he would freeze to death. I was on the phone one night with Shirley and said, What if he

trips and falls and freezes? Someone else
called and told me that there are places
where he can go. He can go sit in a
waiting room. I know that that was a big
help to me. We had phone calls and just
knowing that if I wanted to call anybody
on the list that I could call them at any
time. Everybody was very good. One of
the biggest supports that I had was the
night that Ted overdosed. That was
horrendous. I had never gone through
anything like that. I believe that God
works in mysterious ways. Shirley called
here and she wanted to speak to me.
Chris told her where I was and within...I
look in the waiting room and here was
one of the couples from TOUGHLOVE.
She was in a crisis herself that night and
she couldn't come. And she called this
couple and within a half an hour they
were there. They were sitting and talking
with me. Another one of the girls came
by. After Shirley had her crisis solved,
she was there. Shirley and Sheila sat
with us until four A.M. I just can't tell you
what that meant. I feel like I've got to
give in return, I just can't take all of that.

INTERVIEWER: How about your relatives? What were
their reactions to TOUGHLOVE?

MOM: My family lives three and a half hours
from here. So we haven't had to deal too
much with them. But my father read
about TOUGHLOVE. He's from the older
generation. He likes the theory.

INTERVIEWER: So you felt some support from them?

MOM: In a way, they couldn't understand. How
could you put the kids out of the house?

They didn't understand that. I felt guilty when I talked to them. Doing what I was doing. They didn't understand. They made me feel that I should have been tougher years ago.

INTERVIEWER: You felt blamed?

MOM: Yes. They would not intentionally hurt me that way. But I can read it into what they were saying.

INTERVIEWER: How did you handle it?

MOM: I just basically explained. It's not working the way we are doing it now. Just telling them that the blame game is going to keep me helpless. It was hard. I feel upset when I talk to my parents. My in-laws were even worse. I just handled it by staying away from them. Using the TOUGHLOVE support people. My friends there rather than talking to my family about it. When they saw that it was all working then it was better. They were afraid too. I guess they were afraid for the same reasons that I was afraid.

INTERVIEWER: How about friends? Did you have support from your friends?

MOM: No, not really. Most of our friends have younger children. They really didn't understand.

INTERVIEWER: How do you feel about the community aspects of TOUGHLOVE?

MOM: I think it has a lot to offer the community. I would like to see more of it in the schools.

INTERVIEWER: Have you gotten to know the schools any better?

MOM: Yes. Judge Quinn came to our meeting. The schools agree with it. At first they didn't understand it. They are understanding more and more now. We were going through it and they weren't sure that they agreed with it. More and more as they are realizing what is going on.

INTERVIEWER: Do you feel friendlier toward them now, the schools or the police?

MOM: Yes. I always supported what the police do. Punishments in school, I agree with that. I get frustrated when teachers tell me that my kid is not behaving. I'm not there, I can't make the child behave when they are in school, you have to do that. I would like to see the schools get tougher. Get more discipline. They get away with much too much.

INTERVIEWER: Do you have more supportive people around you now?

MOM: Yes. We've made a lot of friends from TOUGHLOVE.

INTERVIEWER: Would you recommend TOUGHLOVE?

MOM: Absolutely. I think it's great. I just wish that I had had it earlier.

We have included a short interview with Richard Nathan, age sixteen, because he has an understanding of TOUGHLOVE and how it affected his life. We did not include his parents' interview because their story is now so familiar.

INTERVIEWER: I'm speaking with Richard. You are how old now?

RICHARD: Sixteen.

INTERVIEWER: And you are living at home?

RICHARD: Yes.

INTERVIEWER: How did you feel about TOUGHLOVE in the beginning?

RICHARD: I rebelled against it. I didn't want any part of it.

INTERVIEWER: Was TOUGHLOVE helpful to you at all?

RICHARD: Yes, it was through the TOUGHLOVE managers I really found out where I was at. By leaving the house I found out that I had a pretty bad drug problem. Pretty serious drug problem. Through that I was able to get into treatment. I found it really helpful. I appreciated it.

INTERVIEWER: Did it hinder you at all?

RICHARD: In the beginning, yes, before I started recovering on my drug problem, it had a lot of restrictions.

INTERVIEWER: How did it change your parents?

RICHARD: It made them more understanding, they didn't have to blame themselves. I know, today, that a lot of the problems were because of me. Drug addiction and alcohol is a family disease, it affects the other members. My parents had to find a way to cope and TOUGHLOVE is very sufficient. They kind of agreed on where they stood and where I stood. I did quite a bit of supporting for my parents.

INTERVIEWER: Are they different now than they were before TOUGHLOVE?

RICHARD: Yes. They are more understanding. They understand where I'm at today and where I was at before.

INTERVIEWER: Are they stricter or tougher now?

RICHARD: They stand their ground. They are firm on their beliefs. That's where it's at.

INTERVIEWER: Did TOUGHLOVE give you any surprises?

RICHARD: In the beginning, yes.

INTERVIEWER: How do you feel about TOUGHLOVE now?

RICHARD: Very supportive. It has helped my parents a great deal. Myself, I like it too. It makes the parents aware of what's going on out in the street. There are a lot of problems out there.

INTERVIEWER: Have you talked to any other kids about it?

RICHARD: I've talked to other kids in TOUGHLOVE. We all feel about the same.

The Community Service Foundation, which sponsors TOUGHLOVE, is a nonprofit educational organization. For more information about:
   —Parent Support Groups in Your Community
   —TOUGHLOVE Training Workshops
   —Other TOUGHLOVE Educational Materials
   —Joining the Parent Support Network

Contact:
   TOUGHLOVE
   Community Service Foundation
   P.O. Box 1069
   Doylestown, PA 18901

Please send me information about TOUGHLOVE.

Name _____

Address _____

City _____ Zip Code _____

Send to:
   TOUGHLOVE
   Community Service Foundation
   P.O. Box 1069
   Doylestown, PA 18901

ABOUT THE AUTHORS

Phyllis and David York are the founders of TOUGHLOVE. They are licensed therapists and have conducted training workshops for agency administrators, probation officers, counselors, and therapists. It was through trouble with their own three children that the TOUGHLOVE program was developed. The Yorks live in Pennsylvania.

Ted Wachtel is the founder of The Community Service Foundation, the sponsoring agency for TOUGHLOVE, in Sellersville, Pennsylvania.

The authors have completed a second book, *TOUGHLOVE SOLUTIONS*, in which parents and children tell in their own words how TOUGHLOVE's methods have created dramatic and happy solutions for families torn apart by unacceptable adolescent behavior.

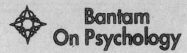

Bantam On Psychology

- ☐ 28037 **MEN WHO HATE WOMEN & THE WOMEN WHO LOVE THEM** Dr. Susan Forward ... $4.95
- ☐ 26401 **MORE HOPE AND HELP FOR YOUR NERVES** Claire Weekes ... $4.50
- ☐ 27376 **HOPE AND HELP FOR YOUR NERVES** Claire Weekes $4.50
- ☐ 26754 **PEACE FROM NERVOUS SUFFERING** Claire Weekes ... $4.50
- ☐ 26005 **HOW TO BREAK YOUR ADDICTION TO A PERSON** Howard M. Halpern, Ph.D. ... $4.95
- ☐ 27043 **THE POWER OF THE SUBCONSCIOUS MIND** Dr. J. Murphy ... $4.50
- ☐ 34367 **TEACH ONLY LOVE** Gerald Jampolsky, M.D. (A Large Format Book) ... $8.95
- ☐ 27087 **CUTTING LOOSE: An Adult Guide for Coming to Terms With Your Parents** Howard Halpern ... $4.50
- ☐ 26390 **WHEN I SAY NO, I FEEL GUILTY** Manuel J. Smith $5.50
- ☐ 28496 **SUPER JOY: IN LOVE WITH LIVING** Paul Pearsall $5.50

ALSO AVAILABLE ON AUDIO CASSETTE

- ☐ 45047 **BREAK YOUR ADDICTION TO A PERSON** Howard Halpern, Ph.D ... $7.95
- ☐ 45080 **MEN WHO HATE WOMEN AND THE THE WOMEN WHO LOVE THEM** Susan Forward, Ph.D ... $7.95
- ☐ 45121 **WHEN AM I GOING TO BE HAPPY? BREAK THE EMOTIONAL BAD HABITS THAT KEEP YOU FROM REACHING YOUR POTENTIAL** Penelope Russianoff, Ph.D ... $8.95
- ☐ 45167 **TEACH ONLY LOVE** Gerald Jampolsky $8.95
- ☐ 45130 **DEVELOP YOUR INTUITION: WOMEN** $7.95

Buy them at your local bookstore or use this page for ordering.

Bantam Books, Dept. ME, 414 East Golf Road, Des Plaines, IL 60016

Please send me the items I have checked above. I am enclosing $_____ (please add $2.00 to cover postage and handling). Send check or money order, no cash or C.O.D.s please. (Tape offer good in USA only.)

Mr/Ms _____

Address _____

City/State _____ Zip_____

ME-2/90

Please allow four to six weeks for delivery.
Prices and availability subject to change without notice.

DON'T MISS
THESE CURRENT
Bantam Bestsellers

Special Offer
Buy a Bantam Book
for only 50¢.